As You Like It, Much Ado About Nothing,
and *Twelfth Night, or What You Will*

An Annotated Bibliography of Shakespeare Studies
1673–2001

PEGASUS SHAKESPEARE BIBLIOGRAPHIES

General Editor
RICHARD L. NOCHIMSON
Yeshiva University

As You Like It, Much Ado About Nothing, and *Twelfth Night, or What You Will*

An Annotated Bibliography of Shakespeare Studies
1673–2001

Edited by
MARILYN L. WILLIAMSON

Pegasus Press
FAIRVIEW, NC
2003

© Copyright 2003
Pegasus Press
101 BOOTER ROAD
FAIRVIEW, NORTH CAROLINA 28730

www.pegpress.org

Library of Congress Cataloguing-in-Publication Data

As you like it, Much ado about nothing, and Twelfth night, or, What you will : an annotated bibliography of Shakespeare studies / edited by Marilyn L. Williamson.
      p. cm. — (Pegasus Shakespeare bibliographies)
Includes bibliographical references and index.
  ISBN 1-889818-35-6
  1. Shakespeare, William, 1564-1616. As you like it—Bibliography.
2. Shakespeare, William, 1564-1616. Much ado about nothing—Bibliography.
3. Shakespeare, William, 1564-1616. Twelfth night—Bibliography.
I. Williamson, Marilyn L., 1927- II. Series.
Z8812.A8 A8 2003
[PR2803]
018'.8223'3—dc21

                                                    2002156341

Cover illustration: From *Kemps nine daies wonder*, 1600. By permission of the Folger Shakespeare Library.

This book has been typeset in Garamond
at Pegasus Press and has been made to last.
It is printed on acid-free paper
to library specifications.

Printed in the United States of America.

CONTENTS

Preface   vii
    List of Abbreviations   x

I. Editions of Shakespeare's Plays and Basic Reference Works

    A. Single-Volume Editions of Shakespeare's Plays   1
    B. Multi-Volume Editions of Shakespeare's Plays   4
    C. Basic Reference Works for Shakespeare Studies   8

II. The Middle Comedies as a Group

    A. Influences; Sources; Historical and Intellectual
        Backgrounds; Topicality   18
    B. Language and Linguistics   23
    C. Criticism   24
    D. Stage History and Performance Criticism   35
    E. Pedagogy   39
    F. Collections   41
    G. Bibliographies   42

III. *As You Like It*

    A. Editions   44
    B. Date and Text   45
    C. Influences; Sources; Historical and Intellectual
        Backgrounds; Topicality   46
    D. Language and Linguistics   52
    E. Criticism   53
    F. Stage History and Performance Criticism   57
    G. Adaptations   63
    H. Collections   64
    I. Bibliography and Concordance   67

IV. *Much Ado about Nothing*

    A. Editions   68
    B. Date and Text   70
    C. Influences; Sources; Historical and Intellectual
        Backgrounds; Topicality   70
    D. Language and Linguistics   74
    E. Criticism   76
    F. Stage History and Performance Criticism   82
    G. Adaptations   86
    H. Pedagogy   87
    I. Collections   88
    J. Concordance   89

V. *Twelfth Night, or What You Will*

    A. Editions   90
    B. Date and Text   92
    C. Influences; Sources; Historical and Intellectual Backgrounds;
        Topicality   92
    D. Language and Linguistics   100
    E. Criticism   102
    F. Stage History and Performance Criticism   112
    G. Adaptations   116
    H. Pedagogy   117
    I. Collections   117
    J. Bibliography and Concordance   119

Index I: Authors and Editors (Sections II–V)   120
Index II: Subjects (Sections II–V)   125

PREFACE

The twelve volumes of this series, of which this is the ninth, are designed to provide a guide to secondary materials on Shakespeare not only for scholars but also for graduate and undergraduate students and for college and high school teachers. In nine of the twelve volumes, entries will refer to materials that focus on individual works by Shakespeare; a total of twenty-five plays, plus *The Rape of Lucrece*, will be covered in these volumes. The remaining three volumes will present materials that treat Shakespeare in more general ways. This is a highly selective bibliography. While making sure to represent different approaches to the study of Shakespeare, the editors are including only work that is either of high quality or of great influence.

In this volume, entries for the works included are numbered consecutively through the volume. Within each subsection, entries are organized alphabetically by author or editor. Each entry contains the basic factual information and a brief annotation. Since inclusion of an item in this volume implies a positive evaluation, the annotations are designed to be primarily descriptive. Evaluations that could not be resisted appear at the end of the annotation.

The organization of this volume is as follows.

Section I, which will be essentially the same in all twelve volumes, contains those editions and general reference works that in the collective opinion of the editors are most basic to the study of Shakespeare. The annotations in this section have been written by the following series editors: Jean E. Howard, Clifford C. Huffman, John S. Mebane, Richard L. Nochimson, Hugh M. Richmond, Barbara H. Traister, and John W. Velz.

Section II contains items that deal with the middle comedies as a group, or at least two of the three plays that make up the middle comedies in this volume: *As You Like It*, *Much Ado about Nothing*, and *Twelfth Night*. Sections III, IV, and V are devoted to *As You Like It*, *Much Ado*, and *Twelfth Night* respectively. Sections II–V are subdivided, and the kinds of works included in these subsections are described in the table of contents. Items that could fit in more than one subsection are referenced at the end of the subsections in which they are not listed. At the end of many annotations, the reader will find references to additional items (with authors' names) that pertain to a topic in the item. Using these references, together with the subject index, the reader may see the range of items included on any particular topic of interest.

Sections II-V contain subsections titled "Collections," in which are listed works that gather previously published or original materials about one or more plays. In each case, names of authors included are listed, as well as names of whole texts in the collection. When an item included in this volume has been reprinted in a collection, the reader is alerted to that fact by the number of the item after the author's name in the annotation, as well as by "repr. in" with the name and number of the collection given after the citation of the item.

Sections III, IV, and V have a subsection, "Adaptations," which includes works that are based on Shakespeare's plays but alter them so substantially as to be independent artifacts. Films and stage productions that present themselves as representations of Shakespeare's work have a different status, and commentary on them is included in subsections on "Stage History and Performance Criticism" for each of the comedies.

Within the entries, numbers prefaced by "no." indicate cross-references; other numbers in parentheses are page numbers or act, scene, and line numbers of the passage discussed (e.g., 2.3.1–5). Act, scene, and line numbers are taken from the Bevington *Complete Works of Shakespeare* (no. 1).

Abbreviations are listed on the following page.

The editors wish to thank their spouses and colleagues for help in compiling this volume. They also wish to thank William C. Carroll, who was originally slated to edit this volume, who contributed some of the annotations and much helpful advice

Marilyn L. Williamson
Richard L. Nochimson
September 2002

Abbreviations

AYL	*As You Like It*
chap., chaps.	chapter(s)
ed., eds.	edited by/editor(s)
e.g.	for example
et al.	and others
F1	First Folio
i.e.	that is
Matt.	*Matthew*
Much Ado	*Much Ado about Nothing*
no., nos.	number(s)
p., pp.	page(s)
Q	quarto
repr.	reprint/reprinted
TN	*Twelfth Night*
trans.	translated by
Univ.	University
vol., vols.	volume(s)

I. EDITIONS AND REFERENCE WORKS

A. Single-Volume Editions.

1. Bevington, David, ed. *The Complete Works of Shakespeare.* Updated 4th edition. New York: Addison Wesley Longman, 1997.

Bevington's *Complete Works* includes 38 plays and the nondramatic poems. Introductions, aimed at a broad audience, focus upon questions of interpretation. The general introduction discusses social, intellectual, and theatrical history; Shakespeare's biography and his career as a dramatist; his language and versification; editions and editors of Shakespeare; and the history of Shakespearean criticism. Appendices include discussions of canon, dates, and early texts; brief summaries of sources; and performance history. There are genealogical charts, maps, and a selected bibliography. Emendations of the copy text are recorded only in an appendix; they are not bracketed in the texts of the plays. Spelling is modernized unless an exception is necessary for scansion, to indicate a pun, or for other reasons discussed in the preface. Notes appear at the bottom of the column. Speech prefixes are expanded. Illustrations include photographs from recent performances. Features ranging from the clarity and high quality of the introductions to the readability of the typeface combine to make the texts in this edition admirably accessible to students and general readers. Available with this edition are the BBC's CD-ROM programs on *Macbeth* and *A Midsummer Night's Dream*. These multimedia resources provide the full text and complete audio recordings; footnotes; word and image searches; sources; comments and audio-visual aids on plot, themes, language, performance history, historical background, and characterization; print capability; and clips from film and video performances. A *Teacher's Guide* to the CD provides suggestions for assignments and classroom use.

2. Evans, G. Blakemore, et al., eds. *The Riverside Shakespeare.* 2nd edition. Boston: Houghton Mifflin, 1997.

This edition includes 39 plays, the nondramatic poems, and segments of *Sir Thomas More*. Introductions by Herschel Baker (histories), Frank Kermode (tragedies), Hallett Smith (romances and nondramatic poems),

Anne Barton (comedies), and J. J. M. Tobin ("A Funeral Elegy" by W. S. and *Edward III*) discuss dates, sources, and major interpretive issues. Harry Levin's general introduction discusses Shakespeare's biography, artistic development, and reputation; intellectual backgrounds; Renaissance playhouses and theatrical conventions; Elizabethan English; and stylistic techniques. Heather Dubrow provides an analytical survey of twentieth-century Shakespeare criticism. Evans provides an introduction to textual criticism. Appendices include a history of Shakespearean performance by Charles H. Shattuck and William T. Liston; substantial excerpts from historical documents related to Shakespeare's life and works, including some early responses to the plays; "Annals, 1552–1616," a listing in four parallel columns of events in political history, Shakespeare's biography, theater history, and nondramatic literature; a selected bibliography; indexes; and a glossary. Emendations of the copy text are enclosed in square brackets, and each play is followed by a summary discussion of editorial problems and by textual notes listing the sources of all emendations. Spelling is modernized except for "a selection of Elizabethan spelling forms that reflect ... contemporary pronunciation" (67). Notes appear at the bottom of the column. The volume includes numerous illustrations, including color plates. While the *Riverside* has many features aimed at general readers, the impressive textual apparatus, Evans's fine discussion of textual criticism, and the collection of documents make this edition of special interest to advanced graduate students and to scholars.

3. Greenblatt, Stephen, Walter Cohen, Jean E. Howard, and Katharine Eisaman Maus, eds. *The Norton Shakespeare, Based on the Oxford Edition*. New York: Norton, 1997.

This edition includes 38 plays (including quarto, folio, and conflated texts of *King Lear*) and the nondramatic poems, including works of uncertain authorship not included in other single-volume editions. The texts (except for "A Funeral Elegy," ed. Donald Foster) are updated versions of those in the modern-spelling, single-volume *Oxford Shakespeare* (1988) produced by general editors Stanley Wells and Gary Taylor with John Jowett and William Montgomery. The *Oxford* edition is based on revisionary editorial principles, including the belief that some texts previously regarded as having limited authority are in reality records (at times highly imperfect) of early authorial versions later revised in the theater. The revised versions are usually chosen as control texts. In the *Oxford*, passages from earlier versions are often reprinted in appendices; the *Norton* prints these passages from earlier versions, indented, within the texts. *The Norton Shakespeare* provides marginal glosses and numerous explanatory notes; the latter are numbered in the text and appear at the bottom of each page. Textual variants are listed after each work. Stage directions added after the 1623 Folio appear in brackets. Greenblatt's general introduction discusses Renaissance economic, social, religious, and political life; Shakespeare's biography; textual criticism; and aspects of Shakespeare's art, including "The Paradoxes of Identity" in characterization and analysis of the "overpowering exuberance and generosity" (63) of Shakespeare's language. Introductions to individual works discuss a range of historical and aesthetic issues. Appendices include Andrew Gurr's "The Shakespearean Stage"; a collection of documents; a chronicle of events in political and literary history; a bibliography; and a glossary. This edition combines traditional scholarship with a focus on such recent concerns as the status of women and "The English and Otherness." Also available is *The Norton Shakespeare Workshop*, ed. Mark Rose, a set of interactive multimedia programs on CD-ROM that can be purchased either separately or in a package with *The Norton Shakespeare*. The *Workshop* provides searchable texts of *A Midsummer Night's Dream*; *The Merchant of Venice*; *Henry IV, Part Two*; *Othello*; *Hamlet*; *The Tempest*; and Sonnets 55 and 138. Students can find analyses of selected passages, sources, essays that illustrate the play's critical and performance history, clips from classic and from specially commissioned performances, selections of music inspired by the plays, and tools for developing paper topics.

4. Hinman, Charlton, ed. *The Norton Facsimile: The First Folio of Shakespeare.* 2nd edition. Introduction by Peter Blayney. New York: W. W. Norton, 1996.

The First Folio of 1623 is a collection of 36 plays made by Shakespeare's fellow actors, Heminge and Condell. *Pericles, The Two Noble Kinsmen,* and the nondramatic poems are not included. Heminge and Condell claim to have provided "perfect" texts, distinguishing them from what they describe as "stolne, and surreptitious copies, maimed, and deformed by the frauds and stealthes of injurious impostors" (A3). While some of the previously published quartos are regarded today as superior versions, the First Folio indeed provides the most authoritative texts for the majority of Shakespeare's plays. It also includes commendatory poems by four authors, including Ben Jonson, and the Droeshout portrait of Shakespeare. During the two years that the 1623 edition was in press, corrections were made continually, and the uncorrected pages became mingled with corrected ones. In addition, imperfections of various sorts render portions of numerous pages difficult or impossible to read. Hinman has examined the 80 copies of the First Folio in the Folger Shakespeare Library and selected the clearest versions of what appear to be the finally corrected pages. In the left and right margins, he provides for reference his system of "through line numbering," by which he numbers each typographical line throughout the text of a play (the verse and prose of the play as well as all other material such as scene headings and stage directions). In a page from *King John*, for example, which includes what might otherwise be referred to as 3.1.324 through 3.3.74 (this form of reference appears in the bottom margin), the through line numbers run from 1257 to 1380. Appendix A presents some variant states of the Folio text, and Appendix B lists the Folger copies used in compiling this edition. Hinman's introduction discusses the nature and authority of the Folio, the printing and proofreading process, and the procedures followed in editing the facsimile, explaining, among other points, the advantages of through line numbering. Blayney's introduction updates Hinman's discussions of such matters as the status of quarto texts, the types of play-manuscripts available to printers, and the printing and proofreading processes. Blayney also discusses the theory that, since different versions of a given play may represent authorial or collaborative revisions, in such cases there is no "ideal text." No interpretive introductions or glosses are provided. While some valuable facsimiles of quarto versions are available, the Hinman First Folio is clearly an excellent place to begin one's encounter with early printed texts that are not mediated by centuries of editorial tradition.

B. Multi-Volume Editions.

5. Barnet, Sylvan, general ed. *The Signet Classic Shakespeare.* New York: Penguin.

Originally edited in the 1960s, the Signet series was updated in the 1980s; newly revised volumes began to appear in 1998. The 35-volume series includes 38 plays and the nondramatic poems. Collections entitled *Four Great Comedies, Four Great Tragedies,* and *The Sonnets and Nondramatic Poems* are available. Each volume in the newly revised series includes a general introduction with discussions of Shakespeare's biography, including the "anti-Stratfordian" authorship phenomenon; Shakespeare's English; Elizabethan theaters; "Shakespeare's Dramatic Language: Costumes, Gestures and Silences; Prose and Poetry"; editorial principles; and the staging of Shakespeare's plays, including consideration of the concept of the play as a collaboration among the playwright, theatrical ensemble, and audience. Spelling is generally modernized, and speech prefixes are expanded. Explanatory notes appear at the bottom of each page. Appendices contain textual notes, discussion of (and often excerpts from) sources, several critical essays, a survey of each play's performance history, and a bibliography. Although introductions in this series are written for beginning students, the substantial selection of distinguished critical essays is useful for more advanced students, as well.

6. **Bevington, David,** ed. David Scott Kastan, James Hammersmith, and Robert Kean Turner, associate eds. *The Bantam Shakespeare*. New York: Bantam, 1988.

In 1988, 37 plays and the nondramatic poems were published in the 29 volumes of *The Bantam Shakespeare*. Collections entitled *Four Comedies* and *Four Tragedies* are available. Texts, explanatory notes (at the bottom of each page), and interpretive introductions are similar to those of Bevington's *Complete Works of Shakespeare* (see no. 1). Included in the Bantam series are brief performance histories of individual plays and Joseph Papp's forewords on Shakespeare's enduring appeal. Each volume includes a one-page biography of Shakespeare and an introduction to Elizabethan playhouses. Appendices include concise discussions of dates and early texts, textual notes, substantial excerpts from sources, and a brief annotated bibliography. While this series necessarily excludes some of the historical information found in the *Complete Works*, the forewords by an eminent producer/director and the well-written performance histories are engaging features, especially appropriate for students and general readers.

7. **Brockbank, Philip,** founding general ed. Brian Gibbons, general ed. A. R. Braunmuller, associate general ed. *The New Cambridge Shakespeare*. Cambridge: Cambridge Univ. Press, 1982—.

The New Cambridge series will eventually include 39 plays (with *The Reign of Edward III*) and the nondramatic poems. So far, 41 volumes have appeared; among these are two separate editions (one based on an early quarto) of *King Lear*, of *Hamlet*, of *Richard III*, and of *Henry V*. Introductions discuss date, sources, critical history and interpretive issues, staging, and performance history (with numerous illustrations). Discussion of the text precedes each play, and more detailed textual analysis sometimes appears in an appendix. All volumes include a selected bibliography. Spelling is generally modernized; speech prefixes are expanded. Textual notes signaling departures from the copy text and extensive explanatory notes appear at the bottom of each page. Designed for students and scholars, *The New Cambridge Shakespeare* provides more detailed attention to stagecraft and performance history than most other editions. This series succeeds *The New Shakespeare*, edited by Arthur Quiller-Couch and John Dover Wilson.

8. Knowles, Richard, and Paul Werstine, general eds. Robert K. Turner, senior consulting editor. *A New Variorum Edition of Shakespeare.* New York: Modern Language Association.

From 1871 to 1928 H. H. Furness, Sr., and H. H. Furness, Jr., published 19 works of the Variorum Shakespeare. Since 1933, nine new editions have appeared in the MLA series. The completed 40-volume variorum will contain 38 plays and the nondramatic poems. Each volume provides an old-spelling text and a collation of significant emendations from previous editions. Explanatory notes (printed below the textual notes at the bottom of each page) try to record all important previous annotation. Appendices include discussions of a play's text and date. Recent volumes survey the history of criticism and performance and refer to a substantial bibliography; early volumes include excerpts from previous criticism. Sources and analogues are discussed and reprinted. As compilations of scholarship, criticism, and textual analysis, these volumes represent a significant resource for scholars and teachers.

9. Mowat, Barbara A., and Paul Werstine, eds. *The New Folger Library Shakespeare.* New York: Pocket Books, Washington Square Press, 1992—.

Twenty-seven volumes of the New Folger series, which replaces *The Folger Library General Reader's Shakespeare*, appeared between 1992 and 2002. Several new titles will come out each year until the series of 38 plays and the nondramatic poems is complete. Each volume provides a brief initial comment on the play followed by basic introductions to Shakespeare's language and style, his biography, Elizabethan theaters, early editions, and the editorial principles of the series. Half brackets enclose emendations of the copy text; in some volumes square or pointed brackets indicate the sources of passages that appear (for example) only in the folio or an earlier quarto. Explanatory notes appear on pages facing the text, textual notes in an appendix. Spelling is selectively modernized, and speech prefixes are expanded. For each play a different critic offers the "Modern Perspective" that follows the text. A brief annotated bibliography focuses mostly on recent approaches to the play; standard works on language, biography, theatrical setting, and early texts also appear. While this series aims at the broadest possible audience, the clarity and helpfulness of its introductions and explanatory notes make it especially well suited for beginning students.

EDITIONS AND REFERENCE WORKS 7

10. **Proudfoot, Richard, Ann Thompson, and David Scott Kastan,** general eds. *The Arden Shakespeare*. Walton-on-Thames, U.K.: Thomas Nelson.

The 40-volume *Arden Shakespeare* includes 38 plays and 2 volumes of the nondramatic poems. The edition is continually updated; although some current volumes are from the 1950s, thirteen plays and the Sonnets have appeared in revised third editions in recent years. Introductions provide extensive discussion of dates, texts, editorial principles, sources, and a wide range of interpretive issues. Extensive textual and explanatory notes appear at the bottom of each page. Appendices typically include additional textual analysis, excerpts from sources, and (sometimes) settings for songs. The Arden series often includes scholarship and criticism that are essential for advanced students and scholars. The complete second edition of the Arden series is available on CD-ROM from Primary Source Media. The CD-ROMs enable one to view the edited texts simultaneously with materials from the following: early quarto and folio editions; Bullough's *Narrative and Dramatic Sources* (no. 15); Abbott's *Shakespearian Grammar*; Onions's *Shakespeare Glossary* (no. 23); Partridge's *Shakespeare's Bawdy*; and a 4,600-item bibliography. The complete Arden set is also available on-line, with additional materials for those works that have appeared in the third edition.

11. **Spencer, T. J. B.,** general ed. Stanley Wells, associate ed. *The New Penguin Shakespeare*. London: Penguin Books.

The 40-volume New Penguin series now includes 37 plays and the nondramatic poems; *Cymbeline* is planned. Dates range from the 1960s through 2001. Introductions discuss a range of interpretive issues and are followed by brief bibliographical essays. Explanatory notes follow the text, succeeded by textual analysis, selective textual notes, and (as appropriate) settings for songs. Spelling is modernized, and speech prefixes are expanded. Emendations of the copy text are not bracketed. The New Penguin will appeal especially to those who wish the pages of the text to be free of annotation.

12. **Wells, Stanley,** general ed. Advisory eds. S. Schoenbaum, G. R. Proudfoot, and F. W. Sternfeld. *The Oxford Shakespeare*. Oxford: Oxford Univ. Press.

Between 1982 and 2002, 27 plays and *Shakespeare: The Complete Sonnets and Poems* were published in the multi-volume *Oxford Shakespeare*. The completed series will include 38 plays and the nondramatic poems. Introductions provide detailed discussion of dates, sources, textual criticism, questions of interpretation, and performance history. Textual notes and extensive commentary appear at the bottom of each page. The commentary and introduction are indexed. Spelling is modernized, and speech prefixes are expanded. The Oxford series is based on revisionary editorial principles, including the belief that some texts previously regarded as of little value are in reality records (at times highly imperfect) of early authorial versions later revised in the theater. The revised versions are usually chosen as copy texts, and appendices sometimes include passages from earlier printed versions. Some appendices include musical settings for songs. Partly because of its editorial principles, this series is of special interest to scholars and advanced students.

C. Basic Reference Works for Shakespeare Studies.

13. Beckerman, Bernard. *Shakespeare at the Globe: 1599–1609.* New York: Macmillan, 1962.

This study of the 29 extant plays (including 15 by Shakespeare) produced at the Globe in its first decade yields information about the playhouse and how Shakespeare's company performed in it. The first chapter, on the repertory system, is based on analysis of Henslowe's diary. Subsequent chapters about the stage itself, acting styles, the dramatic form of plays and of scenes within plays, and the staging derive from study of the Globe repertory. Detailed appendices provide statistics on which Beckerman's analysis partly depends. Beckerman concludes that the style in which these plays were presented was neither symbolic nor what modern audiences would call realistic. Rather, he suggests, passion by the actors was presented within a framework of staging and scenic conventions in various styles according to the needs of particular plays.

14. Bentley, G. E. *The Jacobean and Caroline Stage.* 7 vols. Oxford: Clarendon Press, 1941–68.

Bentley designed his survey of British drama to carry on that of Chambers (see no. 16) and cover the years 1616–42. The 11 chapters in vol. 1 provide detailed information about 11 adult and children's acting companies (1–342); vol. 2 surveys information about actors, listed alphabetically (343–629), with relevant documents reprinted and annotated (630–96), with an index (697–748). Vols. 3, 4, 5 are an alphabetical list, by author, with bibliographical material and commentary, of "all plays, masques, shows, and dramatic entertainments which were written or first performed in England between 1616 ... and ... 1642" (3.v), from "M.A."

to Richard Zouche, with a final section (5. 1281–1456) on anonymous and untitled plays. Vol. 6 considers theater buildings (private, 3–117; public, 121–252; court, 255–88; and two that were only projected, 291–309). Vol. 7 gathers together, as appendices to vol. 6, "scattered material concerning Lenten performances and Sunday performances" and arranges chronologically "a large number of dramatic and semi-dramatic events" of interest to students of dramatic literature and theater history (6.v); it includes a general index for vols. 1–7 (129–390), which has numerous references (344–45) to Shakespeare and his plays.

15. Bullough, Geoffrey. *Narrative and Dramatic Sources of Shakespeare.* 8 vols. London and New York: Routledge and Kegan Paul and Columbia Univ. Press, 1957–75.

This work is a comprehensive compendium of the texts of Shakespeare's sources for 37 plays and several poems. Bullough includes analogues as well as sources and "possible sources" as well as "probable sources." All texts are in English, old-spelling Elizabethan when extant, and in some other cases in the compiler's translation. Bullough includes a separate introduction for each play. In the early volumes, interpretation is largely left to the reader; introductions in the later volumes include more interpretation and tend to be longer. There have been complaints of occasional errors in transcription. The major caveat, however, about using this learned, thorough, and imaginative work concerns what Bullough could not conceivably print: the passages in his sources that Shakespeare presumably read but either chose to omit or neglected to include.

16. Chambers, E. K. *The Elizabethan Stage.* 4 vols. Oxford: Clarendon Press, 1923. Revised 1945; with corrections 1967.

In vol. 1, Chambers provides detailed information about the court (1–234): the monarchs, their households, the Revels Office, pageantry, the mask, and the court play. In the section entitled "The Control of the Stage" (236–388), he covers the struggles between the city of London and the court and between Humanism and Puritanism, and treats the status of actors and the socio-economic realities of actors' lives. In vol. 2, Chambers focuses on the history of 38 different acting companies (children, adult, and foreign) (1–294), gives details, such as are known, about an alphabetical list of actors (295–350), and treats the playhouses (16 public and 2 private theaters), including discussion of their structure and management (351–557). In vol. 3, Chambers surveys the conditions of staging in the court and theaters (1–154), the printing of plays (157–200), and then offers a bibliographical survey, including brief biographies, of playwrights alphabetically arranged, from William Alabaster through Christopher Yelverton (201-518). In vol. 4, Chambers concludes that bibliography with anonymous work (1-74) and presents 13 appendices that reprint or summarize relevant historical documents. Chambers concludes this work with four indices (to plays, persons, places, and subjects) to the four volumes (409-67). In these four volumes, Chambers presents an encyclopedia of all aspects of English drama during the reigns of Elizabeth I and James I up to the date of Shakespeare's death in 1616. A subsequent and detailed index to this entire work was compiled by Beatrice White, *An Index to "The Elizabethan Stage" and "William Shakespeare" by Sir Edmund Chambers*. Oxford: Oxford Univ. Press, 1934.

17. Chambers, E. K. *William Shakespeare: A Study of Facts and Problems.* 2 vols. Oxford: Clarendon Press, 1930. Repr., 1931.

This work is an encyclopedia of information relating to Shakespeare. The principal topics of the first volume are the dramatist's family origins, his relations to the theater and its professionals, the nature of the texts of his plays—including their preparation for performance and publication, and also questions of authenticity and chronology (relevant tables about the quartos and metrics are in the second volume). The data available (and plausible conjectures) concerning all texts attributed to Shakespeare, including poems and uncertain attributions, are then laid out title by title. The second volume cites the significant Shakespeare records then available, including contemporary allusions, performance data, legends, and even forgeries (the last two items are more fully covered in Schoenbaum's *Shakespeare's Lives*). There are comprehensive indices and a substantial bibliography. While it is sometimes necessary to update this book by correlation with Schoenbaum's *Documentary Life* (see no. 25) and other, more recent, texts, Chambers's scholarship has been supplemented rather than invalidated by more recent research, and his work remains a convenient starting point for pursuit of background data on Shakespeare's life and works.

18. De Grazia, Margreta, and Stanley Wells, eds. *The Cambridge Companion to Shakespeare.* Cambridge: Cambridge Univ. Press, 2001.

Following a preface, a "partial chronology" of Shakespeare's life and a "conjectural" one of his works, the nineteen chapters of this new edition of the *Cambridge Companion* (the others were 1934, 1971, and 1986) provide a "broadly historical or cultural approach" instead of the earlier volumes' "formalist orientation" (xv). Ernst Honigmann writes on Shakespeare's life (chap. 1), Barbara A. Mowat discusses the traditions of editing (chap. 2, an essay supplemented by Michael Dobson's survey of page- or stage-oriented editions, chap. 15), Leonard Barkan reviews what Shakespeare read (chap. 3), and Margreta De Grazia skims over some aspects of language and rhetoric (chap. 4). John Kerrigan is specific in his discussion of the poems (chap. 5), a specificity balanced by the more general essays of Susan Snyder on the possibilities of genre (chap. 6), Valerie Traub on Shakespeare's use of gender and sexuality (chap. 9), and David Scott Kastan on the use of history (chap. 11). Social background—the City, Court, Playhouse, etc.—are the subjects of chapters by John H. Astington and Anne Barton (chaps. 7, 8), and Ania Loomba goes farther afield in spotlighting "outsiders" in England and Shakespeare (chap. 10). The last chapters group into two divisions: Shakespeare's posthumous presence in the (British) theater of 1660–1900 (Lois Potter, chap. 12) and in that of the 20th century (Peter Holland, chap. 13), in the cinema (Russell Jackson, chap. 14), on stages and pages worldwide (Dennis Kennedy, chap. 16); and, second, the history of Shakespeare criticism (1600–1900 by Hugh Grady, chap. 17; 1900–2000 by R. S. White, chap. 18). The volume concludes with an annotated list of Shakespeare reference books recommended by Dieter Mehl (chap. 19). Each essay except the last appends its own (further) reading list.

This volume does not precisely replace its immediate predecessor (ed. Wells, 1986, repr. 1991), for the latter's "basic materials ... on Shakespeare's life, ... the transmission of the text, and the history of both criticism and production are still [fortunately] available" (xvi). This availability does not prevent the present volume from printing new essays on some of the same topics; and students, teachers, and scholars may well benefit from comparing the generations—for instance Ernst Honigmann with S. Schoenbaum on Shakespeare's biography, Margreta De Grazia with Inga-Stina Ewbank on Shakespeare and language, Russell Jackson with Robert Hapgood on film (and, in the earlier edition, television) versions of Shakespeare, Hugh Grady with Harry Levin on Shakespeare criticism to about 1900, and R. S. White with the three scholars who wrote three separate essays on his topic, 20th-century Shakespeare criticism. The 1986 edition, then, should be consulted in addition to this new entry.

19. Doran, Madeleine. *Endeavors of Art: A Study of Form in Elizabethan Drama*. Madison: Univ. of Wisconsin Press, 1954.

Doran reconstructs the Elizabethan assumptions about many aspects of dramatic form, defined broadly enough to include genre, eloquence and copiousness, character, and "moral aim." A detailed exploration of classical, medieval, and Renaissance backgrounds makes this a study in historical criticism; however, the cultural context laid out is aesthetic, not ideational. Doran examines the problems of form faced by Shakespeare and his contemporaries—problems of genre, of character, of plot construction—in an attempt to explain the success (or, sometimes, lack of success) of the major dramatists in "achieving form adequate to meaning" (23). Doran's unpretentious, readable study is justly famous as the first book on the aesthetics of Renaissance drama to understand the entire context, to perceive the Renaissance assumptions about dramatic art as a fusion of classical and medieval influences.

20. Gurr, Andrew. *Playgoing in Shakespeare's London.* 2nd edition. Cambridge: Cambridge Univ. Press, 1996.

Gurr focuses on the identity, class, and changing tastes of London playgoers from the opening of the Red Lion in 1567 to the closing of the theaters in 1642. He examines the locations, physical features, price scales, and repertories of the various playhouses, distinguishing particularly between "halls" and "amphitheatres" and rejecting the more common labels "private" and "public." Turning from the theaters, Gurr examines the playgoers, asking such questions as whether they ventured to the playhouses primarily to "hear" a text or to "see" a spectacle. In a final chapter, entitled "The evolution of tastes," he discusses assorted playgoing fashions: from the craze for Tarlton's clowning to the taste for pastoral and romance in the last years of Charles I. Two appendices list identifiable playgoers and references to playgoing during the time period.

21. Gurr, Andrew. *The Shakespearean Stage 1574–1642.* 3rd edition. Cambridge: Cambridge Univ. Press, 1992.

Gurr summarizes a vast amount of scholarship concerning the material conditions of Elizabethan, Jacobean, and Caroline theatrical production. Each of his six chapters provides a wealth of detailed information on theatrical life. The first gives an overview of the place of the theater in urban London from the 1570s until 1642, including an examination of the social status of playwrights, the differences and similarities between the repertories at the open-air amphitheaters (public) and at the indoor playhouses (private), and the changing role of court patronage of theater. Chapter 2 describes the typical composition of London theater companies and their regulation by the Crown. It also gives an historical account of the theatrical companies that at various times dominated the London theatrical scene. In his third chapter, Gurr looks at actors, discussing the famous clowns of the Elizabethan era, prominent tragic actors such as Burbage and Alleyn, and the repertory system within which they worked. The fourth chapter summarizes what is known about the playhouses, including information gleaned from the recent excavation of the remains of the Rose Theater, as well as accounts of the Globe Theater, The Fortune, the hall playhouses, and the Banqueting Hall. Chapter 5 discusses staging conventions and the differences between public and private theaters, and among the various particular theaters, in their use of song, music, clowning, and jigging. Also examined are stage properties and costumes. The final chapter analyzes information about audiences: who went to which kinds of playhouse and how they behaved. Gurr argues that women and all social classes were represented in theatrical audiences, with an increasing tendency in the seventeenth century for the private theaters to cater to a wealthier clientele who demanded a more sophisticated repertory with more new plays. This valuable book concludes with an appendix indicating at which playhouses and by which companies various plays were staged.

22. Kastan, David Scott, ed. *A Companion to Shakespeare.* Oxford: Blackwell Publishers, 1999.

This collection of 28 essays, most with notes and references for further reading, aims to locate Shakespeare in relation to the historical matrix in which he wrote his plays and poems. Following the editor's introduction, the volume is framed by two essays dealing with Shakespeare the man. The first, by David Bevington, deals with what is known, factually, about his life; the last, by Michael Bristol, deals with various myths surrounding the figure of Shakespeare. In between, the book is divided into five sections. The first contains six essays, mainly by historians, dealing with Shakespeare's England, the city of London, religious identities of the period, the family and household structures, Shakespeare and political thought, and the political culture of the Tudor-Stuart period. The second section contains five essays, mostly by literary critics, and discusses readers and reading practices in the early modern period. It includes a general essay on literacy, illiteracy, and reading practices, and four essays focusing on reading, respectively, the Bible, the classics, historical writings, and vernacular literature. The third part of the book deals with writing and writing practices and contains five essays by literary scholars on writing plays, on the state of the English language in Shakespeare's day, on technical aspects of Shakespeare's dramatic verse, on the rhetorical culture of the times, and on genre. These essays are followed by a section on playing and performance. It contains five essays, mostly by theater historians, on the economics of playing, on The Chamberlain's-King's Men, on Shakespeare's repertory, on playhouses of the day, and on licensing and censorship. The final section, consisting of five essays by literary critics, deals with aspects of printing and print culture, including Shakespeare's works in print between 1593 and 1640, manuscript playbooks, the craft of printing, the London book trade, and press censorship. Mixing traditional and newer topics and concerns, *A Companion to Shakespeare* is an up-to-date guide to the historical conditions and the literary and theatrical resources enabling Shakespeare's art.

23. Onions, C. T. *A Shakespeare Glossary*. Oxford: Clarendon Press, 1911. 2nd edition revised, 1919. Repr., with corrections, 1946; with enlarged Addenda, 1958. Enlarged and revised by Robert D. Eagleson, 1986; corrected, 1988.

Onions's dictionary of Elizabethan vocabulary as it applies to Shakespeare was an offshoot of his work on the *Oxford English Dictionary*. Eagleson updates the third edition with new entries, using modern research (now aided by citations from the Riverside edition [see no. 2], keyed by the Spevack *Concordance* [see no. 26]), while conserving much from Onions's adaptation of OED entries to distinguish Shakespearean uses from those of his contemporaries and from modern standard meanings. The glossary covers only expressions that differ from modern usage, as with "cousin" or "noise." It includes some proper names with distinctive associations, such as "Machiavel," and explains unfamiliar stage directions: "sennet" (a trumpet signal). Many allusions are more fully elucidated, as with the origin of "hobby-horse" in morris dances, or the bearing of "wayward" on *Macbeth*'s "weird sisters." This text, which demonstrates the importance of historical awareness of language for accuracy in the close reading of Shakespeare, now has a brief bibliography of relevant texts. It still needs to be supplemented in two areas: information about definite and possible sexual significance of many common and obscure words appears in Gordon Williams's 3-volume *A Dictionary of Sexual Language and Imagery in Shakespearean and Stuart Literature* (1994); often contradictory guidance about the likely pronunciation of Shakespeare's language is provided by Helge Kökeritz's *Shakespeare's Pronunciation* (1953) and by Fausto Cercignani's *Shakespeare's Works and Elizabethan Pronunciation* (1981).

24. Rothwell, Kenneth S., and Annabelle Henkin Melzer. *Shakespeare on Screen: An International Filmography and Videography*. New York: Neal-Schuman, 1990.

This list of film and video versions of Shakespeare seeks to be comprehensive, covering the years 1899–1989, except that it excludes most silent films, referring the reader to Robert Hamilton Ball's *Shakespeare on Silent Film* (1968). It does include "modernizations, spinoffs, musical and dance versions, abridgements, travesties and excerpts" (x). The introduction, by

Rothwell, offers an overview of screen versions of Shakespeare (1–17). The body of the work, with over 675 entries (21–316), is organized by play, listed alphabetically, and within each play chronologically. Represented are 37 plays and the *Sonnets*. *Pericles* and *Timon of Athens* appear only in the BBC versions in "The Shakespeare Plays" series. For *Hamlet* we have 87 entries. Included also are another 74 entries (317–35) for documentaries and other "unclassifiable" films and videos that present Shakespeare in some form, such as John Barton's "Playing Shakespeare" series and James Ivory's film, *Shakespeare Wallah*. The sometimes quite extensive entries include information about and evaluation of the production, and an attempt to provide information about distribution and availability. The work concludes with a useful selected bibliography with brief annotations (337–45), a series of helpful indices (349–98), and a list of the names and addresses of distributors, dealers, and archives (399–404).

25. Schoenbaum, S. *William Shakespeare: A Compact Documentary Life.* Oxford: Oxford Univ. Press, 1977. Repr., with corrections, 1978.

An abridged version of Schoenbaum's massive documentary study of Shakespeare published by Oxford in 1975, the *Compact Documentary Life* traces all textual evidence about Shakespeare chronologically from his grandfather's generation up to the deaths of Shakespeare's surviving family members. Legends for which there is no specific documentation—such as the deer-poaching incident—are examined for probability on the basis of surviving materials. Where appropriate, Schoenbaum juxtaposes biographical details with specific passages in Shakespeare's works. Amply illustrated and annotated, this work, unlike Schoenbaum's earlier, larger version and his later (1981) *William Shakespeare: Records and Images*, refers to documents but generally does not reprint them.

26. Spevack, Marvin. *The Harvard Concordance to Shakespeare.* Cambridge: Belknap Press of Harvard Univ. Press, 1973.

This text covers the total of 29,066 words (including proper names) used by Shakespeare in his plays and poems, in the modern-spelling text of *The Riverside Shakespeare* (see no. 2). Stage directions appear in another volume. Contexts are omitted for the first 43 words in order of frequency, mostly pronouns, prepositions, conjunctions, auxiliary verbs, and articles. Individual entries distinguish between prose and verse, and between total and relative frequencies. The modern spelling is not enforced with proper names or significant Elizabethan divergencies: "embassador-ambassador." While the cited context of each use is normally the line of text in which it appears, other limits occur when the sense requires further wording.

This concordance helps to locate specific passages and also invites subtler research uses, such as study of the recurrence of words in each play: thus the continuity of *Henry VIII* from *Richard III* appears in their shared distinctive use of certain religious terms. Similarly, accumulated references show the divergence or consistency of meaning or associations for particular terms (Shakespeare's references to dogs are unfavorable). In using this text, one must remember that variant spellings or forms of speech may conceal recurrences of words with the same root or meaning (guilt, gilt, guilts, guilty, guiltily, guiltless), while similar spellings of the same word may have contrasting senses (your grace [the Duke] of York, the grace of God, external grace). The provided contexts reveal the complications, but often are too brief to ensure exact interpretation of a word. The magnitude of the effort involved in this concordance indicates the research gain from electronic procedures, which also permit many permutations of its data, as seen in the nine volumes of Spevack's *A Complete and Systematic Concordance to the Works of Shakespeare* (1968–80).

27. Styan, J. L. *Shakespeare's Stagecraft*. Cambridge: Cambridge Univ. Press, 1967. Repr., with corrections, 1971.

Styan's book explores how Shakespeare's plays would have worked, theatrically, on the Elizabethan stage. Beginning with a discussion of the kind of stage for which Shakespeare wrote and of the conventions of performance that obtained on that stage, Styan then devotes the bulk of his attention to Shakespeare's handling of the visual and aural dimensions of performance. He argues that the scripts guide actors in communicating aurally, visually, and kinetically with an audience. Topics considered include gesture, entrances and exits, the use of downstage and upstage playing areas, eavesdropping encounters, the visual orchestration of scenes involving one or several or many characters, the manipulation of rhythm and tempo, and variations among stage voices. The final chapter, "Total Theater," discusses the inseparability of all the elements of Shakespeare's stagecraft in the shaping of a theatrical event aimed at provoking and engaging the audience's fullest response. The book makes a strong case for studying Shakespeare's plays as flexible blueprints for performance that skillfully utilize and transform the stagecraft conventions of the Elizabethan theater.

Note on Bibliographies

In addition to the above works, readers should be aware of the various bibliographies of Shakespeare studies. Among the most valuable are Stanley Wells, *Shakespeare: A Bibliographical Guide*, Oxford: Clarendon Press, 1990; David M. Bergeron and Geraldo U. De Sousa, *Shakespeare: A Study and Research Guide*, 3rd edition, Lawrence: Univ. Press of Kansas, 1995; Larry S. Champion, *The Essential Shakespeare: An Annotated Bibliography of Major Modern Studies*, 2nd edition, New York: Hall, 1993. Thorough bibliographies for each of a gradually increasing number of plays have been appearing since 1980 in the Garland Shakespeare Bibliographies, general editor William L. Godshalk. An important specialized bibliography is John W. Velz, *Shakespeare and the Classical Tradition: A Critical Guide to Commentary, 1660–1960*, Minneapolis: Univ. of Minnesota Press, 1968 (available on-line). In the special area of Shakespearean pedagogy, a useful (although brief) bibliography appears in Peggy O'Brien, "'And Gladly Teach': Books, Articles, and a Bibliography on the Teaching of Shakespeare," *Shakespeare Quarterly* 46 (1995): 165–72. For information on new materials on the study of Shakespeare, readers should consult the annual bibliographies published by *Shakespeare Quarterly* (*World Shakespeare Bibliography*, also available on line), *PMLA* (*The MLA International Bibliography*, also available on-line and on CD-ROM), the Modern Humanities Research Association (*Annual Bibliography of English Language and Literature*, available on-line), and the English Association (*The Year's Work in English Studies*). Ph.D. theses on Shakespeare are listed in *Dissertation Abstracts International*, which is also available on-line.

II. THE MIDDLE COMEDIES AS A GROUP

A. Influences; Sources; Historical and Intellectual Backgrounds; Topicality.

28. Barber, C. L. *Shakespeare's Festive Comedy: A Study of Dramatic Form and Its Relation to Social Custom.* Princeton: Princeton Univ. Press, 1959. Selections repr. in Bloom (no. 149), Halio (no. 150), Scott (no. 151), King (no. 287), Palmer (no. 288), and Wells (no. 289).

This study deals with comedies that follow the festive pattern: *Love's Labor's Lost, Midsummer Night's Dream, Merchant of Venice, 1 & 2 Henry IV, As You Like It,* and *Twelfth Night.* According to Barber, these works have a saturnalian structure that drives through holiday release to value clarification, with which the characters return to everyday life. Barber stresses the relation of the drama to its folkloric roots in community festivals and holiday rituals; he claims that Thomas Nashe's *Summer's Last Will and Testament* (1592-3) is a prototype for festive comedy, and in *As You Like It* the Forest is that place of liberty "where the folly of romance can have its day" (223). Barber believes that participation in love and detachment from it—two attitudes embodied in the other lovers—are reconciled in Rosalind with her mockery of her own deepening love. Humor maintains judgment and proportion about deep experience. For Barber, most of the plays called comedies are really romances, with certain comic accompaniment. In *Twelfth Night* Barber sees the reversal of sexual roles as renewing relations Barber regards as normal. Olivia's attraction to Cesario's feminine qualities brings her from timidity to maturity as a woman, and Orsino is prepared to shift his affections by his sensitivity to the woman behind the disguise. "The effect of moving back and forth from women to sprightly page is to convey how much the sexes differ yet how much they have in common, how everyone who is fully alive has qualities of both" (247). Barber compares the two households of *Twelfth Night*: "Throughout the play a contrast is maintained between the taut, restless, elegant court, where people speak a nervous verse, and the free-wheeling household of Olivia, where ... people live in an easy-going prose. The contrast is another version of the pastoral" (252). Malvolio "is not hostile to holiday because he is a Puritan; he is like a Puritan because he is hostile to holiday" (256). This book has been among the most influential for the plays with which it deals.

29. Belsey, Catherine. "Disrupting sexual difference: meaning and gender in the comedies." In *Alternative Shakespeares*, ed. John Drakakis, 166-90. London: Methuen, 1985.

Belsey argues that Shakespeare's comedies explore the margins of sexual difference, which may be disruptive, dangerous, but pleasurable. In *As You Like It* "Rosalind is so firmly in control of her disguise that the emphasis is on the pleasures rather than the dangers implicit in the transgression of sexual difference" (184). Belsey claims this is also true of Viola as she talks to Orsino about her father's daughter. The point is "to define through the internalization of difference a plurality of places, of possible beings, for each person in the margins of sexual difference which a metaphysical sexual polarity obliterates" (189).

30. Billington, Sandra. *A Social History of the Fool*. New York: St. Martin's Press, 1984.

Billington expands the history of fools from their medieval origins through the much-studied era from 1500 to 1620 to the late nineteenth century. Billington claims that fools were part of seasonal celebrations in the British rural countryside throughout the Middle Ages. Fools became famous in the Tudor and Stuart courts and stage, but then moved back to fairgrounds in the seventeenth century, where, according to Billington, they survived in seasonal entertainments—outdoors in summer and indoors at Christmas. For other comments on fools, see also Evans (no. 31), Welsford (no. 37), Wilcher (no. 65), and Goldsmith (no. 121).

31. Evans, Gareth Lloyd. "Shakespeare's Fools: The Shadow and the Substance of Drama," *Shakespearian Comedy*, ed. J. R. Brown and Bernard Harris, 142-59. Stratford-upon-Avon Studies, 14. London: Edward Arnold, 1972.

From the abundant literature on fools, Evans generalizes about fools as figures in literature. They are difficult to place in social hierarchies, he says: fools, who inhabit aristocratic courts, are a law unto themselves; they have an accepted right to speak their minds, yet can be punished for it. "The fool's knowledge is of the folly of mankind, the fool's ability to exorcise that folly" (154). For Evans, what the fool says may often seem simple, but it is just as often highly complex, and the fool's involvement in the action is always peripheral: "Although at hazard, he is still more free than anyone else to speak because he is relatively uncommitted to any close association with any thing or anyone" (155). Evans argues that the coming of Robert Armin to Shakespeare's company in 1599 meant that Shakespeare could create the particular idiom of fooling for Touchstone and Feste with confidence that Armin could play the parts effectively. "The arrival of the Fool immediately heightened Shakespeare's awareness of the contrast between the created dream and ever-incipient reality" (153). For other comments on fools, see also Billington (no. 30), Welsford (no. 37), Wilcher (no. 65), and Goldsmith (no. 121).

32. **Frye, Northrop.** "The Mythos of Spring: Comedy." In *Anatomy of Criticism: Four Essays*, 163–86. Princeton: Princeton Univ. Press, 1957. Selections repr. in Davis (no. 210).

Frye contributes two fundamental ideas to the discourse on Shakespeare's comedies. One is the plot structure derived from Greek New Comedy. Frye's New Comedy centers on a young man who desires a young woman, but is blocked from marriage by older authority figures, social status, or money. The hero triumphs over the obstacles at the last minute, and a new society forms around the pair, signaled by a festive occasion. This structure works toward a happy ending, which is often manipulated, but desired by the audience. Frye's emphasis on outcome has been questioned by some critics, such as Ejner Jensen (no. 52). The second idea is a specific characteristic of Shakespeare's romantic comedy derived from "a medieval tradition of the seasonal ritual-play" (182), that is grafted on the New Comedy structure. This is the green world of certain comedies, such as *As You Like It*, in which the action moves from the normal world to the green world and returns transformed by a victory of summer over winter. In *Twelfth Night*, Frye believes, "the entire action takes place in the second world" (185). For a refinement on Frye's idea, see Hawkins (no. 50). These concepts have been influential on the criticism of the comedies, either as articulated frameworks or as unstated assumptions.

33. **Lea, Kathleen Marguerite.** *Italian Popular Comedy: a Study in the Commedia dell' arte 1560–1620, with Special Reference to the English Stage.* 2 vols. Oxford: Clarendon Press, 1934.

The male-female transformations of *As You Like It* and *Twelfth Night* are traced to their Italian roots in 2:179–82. Volume 1 contains description of a typical performance; masks used in production; *scenarii* (scenes or episodes); origins; and companies of players. Relations of the Italian plays to the English are traced through Italian companies' visits to England and allusions to masks and devices in the work of Shakespeare and his contemporaries. Also listed in appendices are verses about the buffoons, Italian drama related to the *commedia*, Venetian performances, masks and actors, *scenarii* with examples, and a bibliography. This early work is still useful.

34. Nevo, Ruth. *Comic Transformations in Shakespeare.* London: Methuen, 1980.

Nevo argues that Shakespeare made a unique form of comedy by combining the Donatan formula for comic plots and the battle of the sexes. The formula specifies five parts and a teleological plot that seeks what is missing at the start. Shakespeare changes the formula by having his protagonists not know exactly what they want. "They discover as they go along" (6). According to Nevo, Shakespeare's other major innovation is giving his characters an inner life and the exploitation of a gap in awareness between the characters and the audience. (See Evans, no. 48.) Therefore, "When the plot is finally resolved by some appropriate recognition which enables objectives to be attained, the *anagorisis* is retrospective as well as immediate for the protagonists and holistic or integrative for the audience.... The audience has more material to unify, to knit into coherence, than any single character. But the approach of the protagonist's knowledge to the level of the audience's at the end of the play is what gives the recognitions of the denouement their telling effect" (8–9). Shakespeare's fools, Nevo says, are composite figures, made up of the buffoon, the ironic wit, and the imposter, all described in Greek tracts about comedy. Nevo reads the middle comedies in light of these theories. "*Much Ado, As You Like It,* and *Twelfth Night* are Shakespeare's Praise of Folly and exhibit an Erasmian transvaluation of values in its most exemplary form—as a battle of the sexes in which neither contender is defeated: each possesses a heroine who is the final product of a long dialectic, during the shifts and turns of which traditional antithetical sexual roles have been challenged, subverted, polarized, reversed, exchanged, to be finally transcended in a new synthesis and a new harmony" (18).

35. Orgel, Stephen. *Impersonations: The Performance of Gender in Shakespeare's England.* Cambridge: Cambridge Univ. Press, 1996.

Orgel seeks to place the uniquely English practice of boys' playing women's roles within the wider cultural framework of gender structures. He proposes a model in which boys defuse anxiety provoked by women, whose sexuality was viewed as uncontrollable and who could make men effeminate. Although the male disguise is a protection for both Rosalind and Viola during the wooing process, Orgel stresses its limits. When the essential femaleness emerges in wooing, "Viola and Rosalind start to feel trapped by their disguises rather than protected by them" (63). Orgel argues that showing the boy in the wife in the Epilogue of *As You Like It* is an example of how the stage practice could allay the anxiety of theater audiences. He also suggests how important costume is at the end of *Twelfth Night*, when Viola's dress must be found to transform Cesario into a woman. For further comments on crossdressing, see Shapiro (no. 36), Hayles (no. 51), Kimbrough (no. 53), Rackin (no. 60), and Howard (no. 97).

36. Shapiro, Michael. *Gender in Play on the Shakespearean Stage: Boy Heroines and Female Pages.* Ann Arbor: Univ. of Michigan Press, 1994.

Shapiro explores the variety of effects that may be found within boy heroines: "unfused, discretely layered gender identities—play-boy, female character, male persona. Any one of them could be highlighted at a given moment because all of them were simultaneously present at some level in the spectators' minds" (4). In *As You Like It*, shifts among the layers are so frequent that they produce for Shapiro the illusion that Rosalind is a unified character. In dealing with *Twelfth Night* Shapiro emphasizes the intimacy of Viola and Olivia, which dramatizes Olivia's deepening passion, as well as the scenes with Viola and Orsino, which, Shapiro claims, "generated anxiety about homoerotic intimacy at the metatheatrical level, between the adult male actor and one of the troupe's apprentices" (161). For homosexuality in *As You Like It*, see Traci (no. 107); for boy actresses, see Orgel (no. 35) and Wikander (no. 282).

37. Welsford, Enid. *The Fool: His Social and Literary History.* New York: Farrar and Rinehart, 1935. Selections repr. in Scott (no. 151).

Welsford's study is historical, tracing how the buffoon moved from life to art in a variety of countries and cultures. The fool is associated with courts of despots, and when they disappear, he disappears, Welsford says. This generalization is disputed by scholars, like Billington, who find fool figures widely represented in many settings. Welsford describes the fool of imagination in a variety of forms: the Lord of Misrule in the holiday festivals, the Feast of Fools, the fool of medieval drama, the ships of fools, and the court fool of Elizabethan drama. Of these Shakespeare's figures are the most developed: "He was the only dramatist of the time to make use of the technical peculiarities of the dramatic tradition which he inherited" (250). For other comments on fools, see Billington (no. 30), Evans (no. 31), Wilcher (no. 65), and Goldsmith (no. 121).

38. Williamson, Marilyn L. *The Patriarchy of Shakespeare's Comedies.* Detroit: Wayne State Univ. Press, 1986.

Williamson argues that patriarchy should be interpreted according to its varied historical meanings. She reads the middle comedies, including

The Merchant of Venice, as comedies of courtship in which a socially superior woman is wooed and won by an impecunious man; during the courtship women are powerful and often control the action, while males may prove errant. Williamson claims that the plays deny male ambition in making profitable marriages and that, although women forgive their mates and dwindle into wives, the cuckoldry theme sounds another kind of female power, even in the subordination of marriage. For further comments on cuckoldry, see Montrose (no. 103), Cook (no. 178), and Fineman (no. 251).

B. Language and Linguistics.

39. Brown, John Russell. *Shakespeare Dramatic Style.* New York: Barnes & Noble, 1971.

Brown includes *As You Like It* and *Twelfth Night* among plays analyzed for the way in which Shakespeare's language creates theater. He gives the reader questions to apply to Shakespeare's words, syntax, rhetorical figures, and metrics. He also gives questions about the stage action and then joins the words and actions. Brown provides the general reader with analytic tools to read Shakespeare's language as carefully as actors must when preparing to perform. Brown analyzes three scenes from *As You Like It* in detail: the wrestling scene (1.2) for Shakespeare's expository method; the mock marriage (4.1) as a climactic encounter that explores a range of moods, capturing Rosalind's excitement and Orlando's reactions to her fantasies; and the masque of Hymen (5.4) with its variety of verse forms and songs. Brown describes in detail how Hymen should deliver his lines in order for the scene to have "its proper weight and solemnity" (101). Brown also analyzes three scenes from *Twelfth Night*: the opening scene, which he says combines lyric simplicity with hints of conflict; the "backstairs" scene (2.3) with Feste, Toby, and Andrew, for its colloquial rhythms; and the gulling of Malvolio (3.4), in which Brown points out the enormous leeway afforded the actor by the lack of stage direction.

40. Elam, Keir. *Shakespeare's Universe of Discourse: Language Games in the Comedies.* Cambridge: Cambridge Univ. Press, 1984.

Elam's "study of the self-consciousness of Shakespeare's language" is useful for specific language exercises and their contemporary and classical contexts. For example, there are detailed comments on pastoralism in *As You Like It*, relating Orlando's poems posted on trees to the Angelica-Medoro episode in *Orlando Furioso*. Elam also connects Malvolio's reading of Maria's letter in *Twelfth Night* to the Renaissance practices of reading Egyptian hieroglyphs and Hebrew words as signs of Celestial Mysteries. Topics of chapters are "Games and Frames," "Performances," "Universes," "Signs," "Acts," and "Figures." Elam includes a very helpful glossary of rhetorical terms.

41. Vickers, Brian. *The Artistry of Shakespeare's Prose.* London: Methuen, 1968.

Vickers deals with the middle comedies in a chapter entitled, "Gay Comedy." According to Vickers, *Much Ado about Nothing* is remarkable for the way plot and wit work together: the Watch's discovery of the crime stems directly from Dogberry's style, which also accounts for the delay in its revelation. In each part of the play, the styles change the dramatic mood. *As You Like It*, according to Vickers, is dominated by witty displays of Rosalind and Touchstone, the play being arranged so that neither has a peer as a sparring partner. *Twelfth Night* has no superfluous wit, as Vickers reads it: "Everything in *Twelfth Night* is organized in coherent terms of situation and character" (239). Vickers sees *Twelfth Night* as a turning point in Shakespeare's comedic practice, for, in the plays that follow, the prose of wit is subordinate to situation and character.

See also no. 140.

C. Criticism.

42. Adelman, Janet. "Male Bonding in Shakespeare's Comedies." In *Shakespeare's Rough Magic: Renaissance Essays in Honor of C. L. Barber*, ed. Peter Erickson and Coppélia Kahn, 73–103. Newark: Univ. of Delaware Press, 1985.

Adelman explores the significance of male bonds in an extended comparison of *As You Like It* and *Twelfth Night*. *As You Like It*, she argues, "makes its peace with the psychological issues raised by same sex bonding not so much by exploring as by isolating them" (85). The play achieves this, she suggests, through Rosalind's disguise, which promises heterosexual love (Rosalind) while maintaining the male bond (Ganymede). For Adelman, *Twelfth Night* reveals the losses *As You Like It* evades: Antonio loses Sebastian to Olivia without recompense, but at the same time, *Twelfth Night* presents a far richer version of androgyny in the figure of Cesario and in the fantasy of male-female identical twins, maintaining it to the end. For more comments about Antonio, see Pequigney (no. 265) and Osborne (no. 276); for more comments about same-sex bonding, see Rackin (no. 60) and Traub (no. 62).

43. Bamber, Linda. *Comic Women, Tragic Men: A Study of Gender and Genre in Shakespeare.* Stanford: Stanford Univ. Press, 1982.

Comedies, Bamber claims, have confidence in women that tragedies lack. "In the comic universe the comic heroine need *not* choose between men; she is therefore without terrors for the masculine self" (115). Bamber denies that comedies lead to self-discovery and uses *Twelfth Night* as an example. She sees Olivia as "perfectly attuned to comic values right from the start" (132). Bamber asserts, "Orsino's change of allegiance from Olivia to Viola is as daringly conventional, as arbitrary, as unmotivated as anything in the comedies" (133).

44. Barton, Anne. "*As You Like It* and *Twelfth Night*: Shakespeare's Sense of an Ending." In *Shakespearian Comedy*, ed. J. R. Brown and Bernard Harris, 160–80. Stratford-upon-Avon Studies, 14. London: Edward Arnold, 1972. Repr. in Wells (no. 289).

Barton explores the poise and balance of *As You Like It* as the play faces death, claiming that Shakespeare mitigates the violence of his source. The ending accords with this poise, bringing four couples to wedding and "demonstrates Shakespeare's faith in comedy resolutions. It is a triumph of form." (170) *Twelfth Night*, according to Barton, shows a loss of that faith: Sebastian's sudden appearance disrupts the world of revelry and the illusions of the lovers. According to Barton, the lovers remain in Illyria, but the rest of the cast simply disappears from the stage, as Feste's song bridges the play's world and the audience's. This reading was influential on John Barton's production of 1969. For more comments on the end of *Twelfth Night*, see Carroll (no. 221), Everett (no. 250), Hunter (no. 257), and Huston (no. 258).

45. Berry, Ralph. *Shakespeare's Comedies: Explorations in Form.* Princeton: Princeton Univ. Press, 1972.

Berry is a thematic critic who answers both generic criticism and the prevailing positive readings that stress romantic love. So Berry explores the anti-romantic possiblities of *As You Like It*, in which characters exhibit considerable hostility to one another because the good qualities of others menace one's own, from a clash of temperament and values, and from a simple will to dominate. The path "from forest to court is a change of milieu, not a way out of those problems" (195). Berry stresses how the themes of the middle comedies relate to the great tragedies that follow them: "Much of the ground in *Much Ado* he traverses again in *Othello*. The essential difference between the two plays is the attention paid to the problem of evil, as manifest in Iago and Othello—the other problems of 'knowing' are dealt with in much the same way" (174). Berry emphasizes the ironic and somber elements of *Twelfth Night*: "The cynicism of *Twelfth Night* lies in its acceptance of the truths that fantasy need not bring unhappiness, nor exposure to reality happiness" (211-12).

46. Brown, John Russell. *Shakespeare and His Comedies.* London: Methuen, 1957. Selections repr. in Halio (no. 150), Scott (no. 151), and Palmer (no. 288).

Brown's readings are common-sense interpretations. He demonstrates how the characters that Shakespeare adds to his source in *As You Like It* help to define a social disorder which resembles that represented in the history plays. Touchstone shows the audience how "the pastoral world was not an easy substitute for the corrupt court" (147). Jacques, a commentator on the entire action and never a participant, is a voice for Shakespeare's "preoccupation with the ideal of order in society, in Arden, and in love" (157). Jacques makes the audience aware of the limitations of all the characters, even those that the play most endorses. Of *Much Ado about Nothing* Brown says, "The twin stories ... turn on the same point: the very wise and the very uncertain must both learn to trust inward qualities, mere nothings to some other eyes; through a lover's imagination each must recognize inward truth and beauty, and must speak and act from a convinced heart" (118). Brown's criticism has been highly influential, especially in Britain.

47. Champion, Larry S. *The Evolution of Shakespeare's Comedy: A Study in Dramatic Perspective.* Cambridge, Mass.: Harvard Univ. Press, 1970.

Champion acknowledges the differing models of comedy available to Shakespeare, and he tries to define Shakespeare's individuality. He finds it most readily observed "through an investigation of the comic perspective of the plays—in part, at least, the nature of the characterizations and the devices by which the characters are rendered humorous. Such an analysis suggests that Shakespeare's concern was not with different kinds of comedy but rather with plots involving an increasingly complex depth of characterization." (7) Champion deals with *Comedy of Errors, Two Gentlemen of Verona, Midsummer Night's Dream, Much Ado about Nothing, Twelfth Night, All's Well That Ends Well, Measure for Measure, Winter's Tale,* and *Tempest.* For Champion, *Much Ado* is a comedy of identity, in which Beatrice and Benedick are developed characters, who find their identities as they are tricked by others into acknowledgment of their love. The constabulary and the melodramatic subplot are not, for Champion, thematically integrated with the plot of the merry warriors. Champion sees *Twelfth Night* as the only comedy that is successful at integrating narrative with devices that aid characters to understand their true natures.

48. Evans, Bertrand. *Shakespeare's Comedies.* Oxford: Oxford Univ. Press, 1960. Selections repr. in Scott (no. 151), Palmer (no. 288), and Wells (no. 289).

This study focuses on discrepancies among the characters in awareness of the circumstances of the action as the major engine of Shakespeare's designs and the means by which some characters control the world of the play. Evans also analyzes the discrepancies between the awareness of the audience and the characters on stage. In *As You Like It* Evans sees Rosalind as superior in awareness to all those she encounters, not only because of her disguise, but because of her wit. In *Much Ado about Nothing*, Evans says, "All the action is impelled by a rapid succession of 'practices'—eight in all, the first of which is introduced at the end of the opening scene, the last exploited in the final moments" (69). Among the comedies, Evans admires most the practices of *Twelfth Night*, especially Maria's trick on Malvolio: "Exhibiting the seduction of a mind eager to be seduced, the scene surpasses everything resembling it in Shakespeare" (131).

49. Goddard, Harold C. *The Meaning of Shakespeare.* Chicago: Univ. of Chicago Press, 1951. 2 vols. 1: 271-306. Selections repr. in Bloom (no. 149), Scott (no. 151), Davis (no. 210), and King (no. 287).

Goddard views the middle comedies as Shakespeare's farewell to wit. *Much Ado* is full of lies and deceptions and "saturated with this idea of the power of Nothing (of the creative ingredient of the imagination, that is) to alter the nature of things for good or ill" (275); the play is a study of egotism, of which Dogberry is the sublime parody. Goddard is dismissive about *As You Like It*. He stresses the play's artificiality, the lioness, the snake, the religious old man. He has little regard for Jacques or Touchstone, but compares Rosalind to Hamlet in her intellectual range and control of her world. (See Bloom, no. 149.) For Goddard, *Twelfth Night* marks the end of feudalism and is an "intimation of the Puritan revolution with its rebuke to revelry—down even to the closing of the theaters" (295). According to Goddard, Viola and Sebastian rescue the Illyrians from excesses and their aristocracy from decay, and Feste is the one sane figure in the two households.

50. Hawkins, Sherman. "The Two Worlds of Shakespearean Comedy." *Shakespeare Studies* 3 (1967): 62-80.

In order to account for the structure of *Comedy of Errors, Love's Labor's Lost, Much Ado about Nothing,* and *Twelfth Night*, Hawkins adds another pattern to Frye's "green world," (no. 32). Hawkins points out that the structure of the green world applies only to *Midsummer Night's Dream, Two Gentlemen of Verona, Merchant of Venice,* and *As You Like It.* Instead of leaving the sere world for the green world, characters in the first group of plays invade a closed world of sexual antagonism. "The closed world is a metaphor, a symbol for the human heart. The force which knocks at its closed door is love." (69) The happy ending therefore comes from a change of heart. For Hawkins, these comedies represent an acting out of the anti-comic spirit—usually jealousy or narcissism—and fix blame on a scapegoat. Mistakes are more humiliating in the closed world than in the green. Hawkins suggests how the two worlds—green and closed—are constantly reworked and recombined by various authors in a variety of genres.

51. Hayles, Nancy K. "Sexual Disguise in *As You Like It* and *Twelfth Night.*" *Shakespeare Survey* 32 (1979): 63–72. Selections repr. in Scott (no. 151).

Hayles uses the concept of layers of gender to discuss Rosalind and Viola in disguise. Rosalind's layers of disguise allow her to express as Ganymede playing Rosalind the needs of the real Rosalind, which differ from the idealizations and stereotypes that Orlando thrusts upon her. As Ganymede she can reflect upon Phebe's excesses and then trick Phebe into accepting Silvius. The "real" character pierces the disguise in Rosalind's swoon, just as the boy actor reveals himself in Rosalind the wife in the Epilogue, completing the unlayering. The effect of Viola's disguise is to release both Orsino and Olivia from their rigid positions, but only with good fortune in the existence of Sebastian. "The progression from *As You Like It* to *Twelfth Night* shows a shift in emphasis from a *sexual* disguise to a sexual *disguise*" (72). This article begins a continuing discussion of the instability of gender differences, the construction of sex, and the theatrics of crossdressing in the middle comedies also seen in Orgel (no. 35), Shapiro (no. 36), Kimbrough (no. 53), Rackin (no. 60), and Howard (no. 97).

52. Jensen, Ejner J. *Shakespeare and the Ends of Comedy.* Bloomington: Indiana Univ. Press, 1991.

Jensen's readings attend to process, rather than to the ends of comedies, which he sees as over-emphasized by critics under the influence of Frye (no. 32) and Barber (no. 28). Jensen reads *As You Like It* as a series of performances for the audience, which the characters set up for one another. Some are like operatic arias; some are duets. Touchstone and Jacques are the major performers and only topped by Rosalind in her management of the action at the end of the play. In reading *Much Ado about Nothing*, Jensen emphasizes the "merry war" of Beatrice and Benedick at the expense of the Claudio-Hero action, which in his view has been made more dominant by critics than need be. In his discussion of *Twelfth Night*, Jensen accents Shakespeare's masterly design of the action, how he prepares the audience for a character's appearance long in advance. The ready examples are Malvolio cross-gartered and Sebastian, the survivor. "Shakespeare takes all the burden off the question of whether and places it entirely on the question of how" (111). For further comments on dramatic process, see also Champion (no. 47), Jenkins (no. 123), and Howard (no. 275).

53. Kimbrough, Robert. "Androgyny Seen Through Shakespeare's Disguise." *Shakespeare Quarterly* 33 (1982): 17-33. Selections repr. in Scott (no. 151).

This is an early discussion of androgyny that followed Carolyn Heilbrun's *Toward a Recognition of Androgyny* (1973), which deals briefly with Shakespeare's disguised heroines. Kimbrough's thesis is that her disguise allows Rosalind to become "a fuller human self" (23). With Celia she can be one of the girls, with Orlando one of the boys; both can speak to her with a frankness not probable with the opposite sex. With Phebe, Ganymede can expose "the absurdity of social restrictions caused by gender stereotyping" (25). The Epilogue reminds the audience "that while the differences between men and women are important and powerful, we are all most human under the surface" (27). For Kimbrough, Viola feels self-conscious in her disguise and gradually comes to see it as wicked, monstrous, but the disguise allows both Olivia and Orsino to get to know the essential Viola-Sebastian. Olivia and Orsino "are stimulated by her to draw on their androgynous potential for human growth and to develop toward full, whole, integrated selves" (32). The concept of androgyny lost its attractions for feminist critics in the eighties and nineties and was replaced by discussions of gender and the instability of gender identity.

54. Kott, Jan. "Shakespeare's Bitter Arcadia." In *Shakespeare Our Contemporary*, trans. Boleslaw Taborski, 287-342. Garden City: Doubleday, 1966. Selections repr. in Scott (no. 151).

Kott presents a long essay that covers the sonnets and earlier comedies in addition to *As You Like It* and *Twelfth Night*. He consistently stresses the bitter beneath the sweet in the poems and the plays. He claims there is something disturbing in Viola's disguise. "But it is not enough for Cesario-Viola-Sebastian to be acted by one person. That person must be a man. Only then will the real theme of Illyria, erotic delirium or the metamorphosis of sex, be shown in the theatre" (314). In *As You Like It*, Rosalind's disguise represents "the dream of an erotic experience in which one is one's own partner" (323). For Kott, the Forest of Arden is a metaphor for an escape from the limitations of sex: it is a world of madness, mythology, and disguise. The clowns show the bitterness behind the fantasy world, according to Kott. They have ceased to be funny: "Disintegration is their function. They live in a bare world bereft of myths, reduced to knowledge without illusions." (335) Kott has been very influential on directors in search of novel approaches to classic plays.

55. Krieger, Elliot. *A Marxist Study of Shakespeare's Comedies.* New York: Barnes and Noble, 1979. Selections repr. in Scott (no. 151) and White (no. 290).

Krieger reads the multiple meanings of *nature* in *As You Like It* as allowing the play to define class differences benignly: "The opposition between labour and freedom in Arden does not subject one class to another but helps determine those who have 'superior natures' and who 'by nature' should rule" (95). For Krieger, the shepherd has his own kind of superiority in the contentment of his fixed state, and the aristocrats, free from labor and possessed of style, can move anywhere and seem destined by nature to rule. "They express the particular interests of their own class as if these were identical with universal interests" (96). Krieger also analyzes the behavior of four servants in *Twelfth Night*: Viola, Antonio, Maria, and Malvolio. Although Viola and Antonio both provide ideal service, Viola regains her aristocratic status, while Antonio suffers an almost tragic defeat, cast off by Sebastian for an aristocratic marriage. In contrast to Malvolio, Maria earns higher status through giving shape to Sir Toby's aristocratic indulgence. Krieger says that, although Malvolio accepts aristocratic assumptions, he is treated like an object in the trick and punished for his ambition, and the dominant ideology is reinforced by the fact that fortune disposes of benefits according to status. For Krieger's article on *Much Ado about Nothing*, see no. 187.

56. Leggatt, Alexander. *Shakespeare's Comedy of Love.* London: Methuen, 1974. Selections repr. in Scott (no. 151) and Wells (no. 289).

Leggatt deals with *Comedy of Errors, Taming of the Shrew, Love's Labor's Lost, Midsummer Night's Dream, Merchant of Venice, Much Ado about Nothing, As You Like It,* and *Twelfth Night*. He stresses the internal variety of each play, the tensions among the differing styles or dramatic idioms. According to Leggatt, concentrating on plays of romantic love yields a better sense of the variety of Shakespeare's art in dealing with similar material. In *Much Ado about Nothing*, "the action of the Claudio plot, by its very formality, is seen as connected with the basic, familiar rhythms of life. And the love affair of Beatrice and Benedick—so naturalistically conceived, so determined by individual character—is seen, at bottom, as a matter of convention." (182) *As You Like It*, Leggatt says, "is an artifact of illusion, and that is freely admitted—but all we have to do is look at the audience to see the truth of its final vision of humanity walking to the Ark in pairs" (218). In *Twelfth Night*, he says, "The lovers, having engaged our feelings as human beings, are now fixed in a harmony we can believe in only by trusting the power of fantasy; the clowns, stylized in their way at first, have lost some of the immunity of comedy and now present an image of defeat that is uncomfortably real" (253).

57. **MacCary, W. Thomas.** *Friends and Lovers: The Phenomenology of Desire in Shakespearean Comedy.* New York: Columbia Univ. Press, 1985.

Using a psychoanalytic approach, MacCary deals with early comedies, the mature comedies, and *Winter's Tale:* "I am convinced that the ten comedies I shall discuss here are a consideration of the orientation of desire and its constitution of individual identity" (1). In *Much Ado about Nothing* MacCary sees Benedick as loving, in Beatrice, his mirror image, "the most satisfying sexual union" (155), but Claudio never moves beyond the infantile idealization of Hero. In *As You Like It* MacCary says that Rosalind loves Orlando for his simplicity, which gradually changes during their courtship, while he loves her for her complexity as Rosalind-Ganymede. Both thus experience a love deepening from idealization to "the phenomenal type" (176). *Twelfth Night*, for MacCary, brings this pattern to fruition: "There could be no finer figure for Shakespeare's conception of 'mature love': it is love which moves beyond mirroring and idolatry to a point where it can accept change in its object because its subject is not only secure in himself but is himself capable of change, of assimilating to fresh, rich patterns" (189).

58. **Neely, Carol T.** "Lovesickness, Gender, and Subjectivity: *Twelfth Night* and *As You Like It.*" In *A Feminist Companion to Shakespeare*, ed. Dympna Callaghan, 276-98. Oxford: Blackwell, 2000.

Neely explores how lovesickness discourse shapes erotic subjects and represents transgressive love. She concludes, "In *Twelfth Night*, eroticism and gender are detached, destabilizing gender formations and releasing ungendered desires. In *As You Like It*, eroticism remains mapped onto gender but gender roles and desires multiply. Attending to lovesickness in the two plays suggests that the concluding marriages may be less a prescriptive imposition of a hierarchical patriarchy than an accommodation to subjects both male and female who negotiate within culture and ideology to attain their compelling desires." (276)

59. Novy, Marianne. "'An You Smile Not, He's Gagged': Mutuality in Shakespearean Comedy." In *Love's Argument: Gender Relations in Shakespeare,* 21–44. Chapel Hill: Univ. of North Carolina Press, 1984.

Novy explores mutuality and reciprocation in wit and love in *As You Like It, Much Ado,* and *Twelfth Night.* She believes that the trick played on Beatrice and Benedick works because it permits them "to love while seeing themselves as responding only in recompense—not as initiating a request for love with its attendant risk of rejection; they feel assured of mutuality" (27). In *As You Like It,* Petrarchan idealization is, for Novy, the obstacle to mutuality, which is gradually overcome through games and mockery. For Novy, *Much Ado* represents the greatest mutuality in Beatrice and Benedick, who are "capable of being both listener and wit" and therefore they have "a more complex and less asymmetrical love relationship, in which a more complete sharing is possible" (28). In *Twelfth Night* she argues that self-love is the enemy of mutuality because it indulges unrequited love. The mutuality at the end is symbolized in the union of the twins, and, she contends, the play accents the mutuality of the audience and the players in Feste's song.

60. Rackin, Phyllis. "Androgyny, Mimesis, and the Marriage of the Boy Heroine on the English Renaissance Stage." *PMLA* 102 (1987): 29–40.

According to Rackin, gender roles in *As You Like It* and *Twelfth Night* occupy a middle ground between those in Lyly's *Gallathea,* where gender is arbitrary and unreal, and Jonson's *Epicoene,* where gender is a strictly enforced reality. For Shakespeare, according to Rackin, the boy actress's sexual ambiguity becomes a complication in his plots, as with Rosalind's disguise as Ganymede/Rosalind, to be wooed by her beloved, or Viola's disguise leading to Sebastian's marriage to Olivia. Rackin sees the play of gender taking place in the world of art in contrast to the rigidly fixed roles enforced by the antitheatrical tracts of the Puritans. The changes in the portrayal of the transvestite heroines are, for Rackin, a precursor to women's loss of power in the seventeenth century, when gender roles become more rigidly fixed. Shakespeare's heroines "give us a glimpse of a liminal moment when gender definitions were open to play" (38). For further comment on metamorphosis and gender roles, see Carroll (no. 221).

61. Suzuki, Mihoko. "Gender, Class, and the Ideology of Comic Form: *Much Ado about Nothing* and *Twelfth Night.*" In *A Feminist Companion to*

Shakespeare, ed. Dympna Callaghan, 121–43. Oxford: Blackwell, 2000.

Suzuki juxtaposes Shakespeare's comedies with two domestic tragedies, *Arden of Faversham* and *A Warning for Fair Women*, to explore how the genres deal with anxieties about gender and class. She claims that the tragedies hold women responsible for social disorder due to ambition, while *Much Ado* and *Twelfth Night* displace on Don John and Malvolio any anxieties about the unruliness of the women. Suzuki claims that the tragedies, therefore, enact and affirm male fantasies, while the comedies critique those fantasies, demonstrating their cost to women, and acknowledge "the subjecthood of women" (141).

62. Traub, Valerie. *Desire and Anxiety: Circulation of Sexuality in Shakespearean Drama.* London: Routledge, 1992.

Traub contrasts *As You Like It* and *Twelfth Night* in their representation of homoeroticism and the play of desire. She says, "The homoeroticism of *As You Like It* is playful in its ability to transcend binary oppositions, to break into a dual mode, a simultaneity, of desire.... The proceedings of Hymen that conclude the play, once read in terms of the 'mock' marriage which precedes them, enact only an ambivalent closure." (123) In *Twelfth Night*, on the other hand, she contends, "The homoerotic energies of Viola, Olivia, and Orsino are displaced onto Antonio, whose relation to Sebastian is finally sacrificed for the maintenance of institutionalized heterosexuality and generational continuity" (123). Traub's argument is elaborately theorized, using psychoanalytic concepts and feminist cultural materialism to frame her interpretations. For further comments on male-male bonding, see Adelman (no. 42), Pequigney (no. 265), and Osborne (no. 276).

63. Van Doren, Mark. *Shakespeare.* New York: Henry Holt, 1939. Selection repr. in Scott (no. 151) and King (no. 287).

Van Doren may have been the first critic to assert in a developed argument that *As You Like It* presents multiple perspectives on its pastoralism and its love themes, perspectives that critique the themes, but leave them standing, "as much created as destroyed" (128). Van Doren defines precisely the roles that Rosalind, Jacques, and Touchstone play in developing the differing kinds of laughter. It is Rosalind, he says, who is the true philosopher of the play. "Romance has been tested in her until we know it cannot shatter; laughter has made it sure of itself" (134). Van Doren also adds his voice to criticism of *Twelfth Night* that centers the play in Malvolio. He insists that while Viola is Julia (*Two Gentlemen of Verona*) grown to greatness, the confusion of the twins, the two love matches, and the fencing scenes are not what the comedy is about. "Even

Viola, much as we like her, stands a little to one side of the center. The center is Malvolio. The drama is between his mind and the music of old manners" (143).

64. Westlund, Joseph. *Shakespeare's Reparative Comedies: A Psychoanalytic View of the Middle Plays.* Chicago: Univ. of Chicago Press, 1984.

Westlund deals with *The Merchant of Venice, Much Ado about Nothing, As You Like It, Twelfth Night, All's Well That Ends Well,* and *Measure for Measure,* using the Kleinian model to demonstrate how Shakespeare helps his audience transcend the inner conflicts they bring to the experience of the play. According to Westlund, the characters of *As You Like It* achieve autonomy with relative ease because the play expresses a fine balance between the ideal and real. "The freedom of Arden is the liberty to follow one's will within acceptable limits" (89); this is partly demonstrated by the fact that some characters decide to remain in Arden instead of returning to the court. In *Much Ado,* Westlund believes, scheming and manipulation deprive characters of autonomy, and they grow angry at their lack of control over their lives; Beatrice and Benedick overcome their self-love in care for Hero and each other. In *Twelfth Night,* Westlund says, Viola is a means whereby the narcissism of Orsino and Olivia is transformed into action and trust in reality. "The play makes the wish [to idealize] plausible—despite its apparent madness and folly—because the lovers who idealize others actually find them" (119).

65. Wilcher, Robert. "The Art of the Comic Duologue in Three Plays by Shakespeare." *Shakespeare Survey* 35 (1982): 87–100. Repr. in Scott (no. 151).

Wilcher claims that Shakespeare's fools, Touchstone and Feste, reveal much of themselves in the way they spar with those they perceive as social inferiors. Touchstone proves to be out of his element in Arden, especially when he tries unsuccessfully to humiliate Corin and William: "He is exulting in his superior wit for his own and Audrey's benefit, not for ours, and this gives an unpleasant edge to the whole sequence" (93). According to Wilcher, Feste resents being confined to the role of the fool, "to practise an art which he knows is not natural to him" (97), and he reveals this discomfort in scenes with Maria, Olivia, and Viola. For further comment on Feste, see Codden (no. 248), Summers (no. 268), and Greif (no. 274).

D. Stage History and Performance Criticism.

66. Brode, Douglas. *Shakespeare in the Movies from the Silent Era to "Shakespeare in Love."* Oxford: Oxford Univ. Press, 2000.

In a chapter on "Sophisticated Comedy" Brode reviews several films: Branagh's *Much Ado* (1993); Paul Czinner's *As You Like It* (1936) with Elizabeth Bergner and Laurence Olivier; Christine Edzard's *As You Like It* (1992); a Russian version of *Twelfth Night* (1955); and Nunn and Parfitt's *Twelfth Night* (1996). Brode's comments about Shakespeare's texts are idiosyncratic and sometimes wrong, but his discussions of the films are useful.

67. Dawson, Anthony B. *Watching Shakespeare: A Playgoer's Guide.* London: Macmillan Press, 1988. Selection repr. in Tomarken (no. 152).

Dawson writes "with the interests of the playgoer in mind." He has "tried to approach each play from the point of view of key decisions about it that the actors and director must make in order to put it on the stage" (xi). The introduction provides a brief stage history of Shakespearean production for the past 80 years. Dawson stresses the plotlessness of *As You Like It* and its charm. "There is no mistaking that charm, and a production that lacks it is sure to founder" (42). Dawson gives much attention to Jacques, who can be "played in a hundred different ways" (47), and to the complexity of the ending with the masque of Hymen and the Epilogue. Dawson explains that in twentieth-century productions *Twelfth Night* has gone from being a high-spirited romp to a melancholy, autumnal play—which provides "a real gain in our understanding" (51). He stresses the complexity and the many options actors have in performing crucial moments in the action. For Dawson, "*Twelfth Night* presents us with a tangled web of unfulfilled desire, of blind alleys and frustrated hopes" (58). For further comments about changes in productions of *Twelfth Night*, see Berry (no. 271).

68. Gay, Penny. *As She Likes It: Shakespeare's Unruly Women.* London: Routledge, 1994. Selection repr. in Wynne-Davies (no. 211).

Gay studies English performances of *As You Like It, Measure for Measure, Much Ado about Nothing, Taming of the Shrew,* and *Twelfth Night* from World War II to 1990. For *As You Like It*, she covers Glen Byam Shaw's production in 1952; a repeat starring Peggy Ashcroft in 1957; Michel Elliot's production of 1961, starring Vanessa Redgrave; David Jones's production in 1967 with Dorothy Tutin as Rosalind and Janet Suzman as Celia; the National Theatre's all-male production of 1967; Buzz Goodbody's Royal Shakespeare Company production in 1973;

Trevor Nunn's at Stratford in1977; Terry Hand's in 1980; Adrian Noble's production in 1985; and John Caird's in 1989. For *Much Ado* Gay covers John Gielgud's Stratford production in 1949; the Stratford production of 1958, starring Michael Redgrave; Michael Langham's RSC production in 1961; Trevor Nunn's version in 1968; Ronald Eyre's revival in 1971; John Barton's British Raj production of 1976; Terry Hand's version in 1982 with Derek Jacobi as Benedick; Di Trevis's RSC production in 1988; and Bill Alexander's production in 1990. For *Twelfth Night* Gay covers the Shakespeare Memorial production of 1947; Gielgud's production with Olivier and Leigh in 1955; the 1958 version by Peter Hall; the 1966 production with Diana Rigg; John Barton's production in 1969; Peter Gill's version of 1974; Terry Hand's RSC production of 1979; John Caird's in1983; and Bill Alexander's in 1987.

69. Greenwald, Michael. *Directions by Indirections: John Barton of the RSC.* Newark: Univ. of Delaware Press, 1985.

Greenwald gives extended accounts of Barton's productions of *Twelfth Night* from 1969 to 1972 and *Much Ado* in 1976. Barton's *Twelfth Night* stressed the melancholy side of the text, "the last rite of a festive season" (88). Feste is the center of this effect. "This was a play in which everyone was a madman or pretender or both, and in which sanity and frenzy, reality and illusion, were so intermixed that only a jester could hope to distinguish them" (89). Barton's setting emphasized madness and dreams, as did the subdued tones of the costumes. In Barton's interpretation, Olivia is a young girl afraid of life, Viola has an aura of spirituality, Malvolio is the only character who opposes the abdication of common sense on the part of the aristocracy, and Feste's final song signifies that all holidays come to an end. Barton set *Much Ado* in the Indian Raj of Rudyard Kipling. According to Barton's interpretation, the sexual polarization of the officers' club and the female household accounts for the misunderstandings of the plot. Greenwald says, Barton's presentation of a plain wedding in a civil ceremony was not well regarded by critics, nor was Dogberry's condescending attitude toward Indians represented in the production. Despite these objections, the production was regarded, according to Greenwald, as the best since Gielgud's in the fifties. For further comments on Barton's productions, see Mason (no. 199), Berry (no. 271), and Billington (no. 272).

70. Hogan, Charles B. *Shakespeare in the Theatre: A Record of Performances in London, 1701–1800.* 2 vols. Oxford: Clarendon, 1952–57.

Hogan lists London performances of all Shakespeare plays by year and theatre for the period he covers. A second part gives cast lists and other information drawn from promptbooks, playbills, published scripts, and newspapers. In appendices he lists his sources of information and the order of popularity of the plays in the canon, according to number of performances. Hogan also supplies a list of the London theatres active during the period. The information is especially useful because the period covered is one in which Shakespeare's texts were often radically revised. For a discussion of the performance text, see Osborne (no. 277).

71. Jackson, Russell. "'Perfect Types of Womanhood': Rosalind, Beatrice, and Viola in Victorian Criticism and Performance," *Shakespeare Survey* 32 (1979): 15–26.

The three heroines were deemed examples for Victorian womanhood in works by Mary Cowden Clarke, Edward Dowden, George Fletcher, William Hazlitt, Anna Jameson, Charles Knight, and Edward Russell. The theatre, according to Jackson, responded to this idealization with performances of the comedies featuring all the prominent actresses of the time. The performances of Helena Faucit, Ellen Terry, Ada Rehan, Marion Tree, Adelaide Neilson, and Julia Marlowe, among others, are described briefly by their contemporaries.

72. Odell, George C. D. *Shakespeare from Betterton to Irving.* 2 Vols. London: Constable, 1921. Repr. with new Introduction by Robert H. Ball, New York: Dover, 1966.

This extensive account is broken into sections identified with the leading theatrical figure of the time: Betterton, Cibber, Garrick, Kemble, Leaderless Age (1817–37), Macready, Phelps and Kean, Irving. Each section covers scripts, theatres, scenery, and costumes, and offers contemporary comment and background about major productions. For *As You Like It* Odell covers the adaptation *Love in a Forest* (no. 146); the revival of Shakespeare in Garrick's age; productions by Kemble, Macready, and Kean; Lillie Langtry's Rosalind, and Sothern and Marlowe's production of 1907. For *Much Ado about Nothing* Odell covers the adaptations, *The Law Against Lovers* (no. 204) and *The Universal Passion* (no. 205); the revival of Shakespeare in Garrick's age; Kemble's version; Oxberry's version; Macready's interpretation; a production by Kean; a version by Irving; a revival by G. Alexander; and another by Ellen Terry. For *Twelfth Night*, Odell covers the adaptation *Love Betray'd* (no. 283); the revival of Shakespeare in Garrick's age; Bell's version; Kemble's version; Inchbald's version; Reynolds's opera; a revival by Kean; productions by Irving, Daly, Tree, Benson, and the Elizabethan Society.

73. Rothwell, Kenneth S. *A History of Shakespeare on Screen.* Cambridge: Cambridge Univ. Press, 1999.

Rothwell offers extended comments on several films of the middle comedies. They are Paul Czinner's *As You Like It* of 1936 with Laurence Olivier as Orlando and Elisabeth Bergner as Rosalind (which he likes better than do most critics); Yakov Fried's *Twelfth Night* of 1955; Christine Edzard's *As You Like It* in 1992; Trevor Nunn's *Twelfth Night* in 1996; and Kenneth Branagh's *Much Ado* in 1993. Rothwell is more positive in general about the films he discusses than are other commentators.

74. Salgādo, Gāmini. *Eyewitnesses of Shakespeare: First Hand Accounts of Performances 1590–1890.* New York: Barnes & Noble, 1975.

This collection offers excerpts from performance commentaries from the beginning of Shakespeare's career. For each play in the canon, Salgādo includes three or more accounts of productions, some by well-known critics. For *As You Like It*, he presents a description of Peg Woffington's last appearance on the stage, as Rosalind in 1757; a production at Coombe House, an open-air setting, described by Oscar Wilde, with Orlando played by Lady Archibald Campbell in 1885; and a review of Ada Rehan as Rosalind by George Bernard Shaw in 1897. For *Much Ado about Nothing*, Salgādo presents a review of a production by Leigh Hunt in 1808; an account of Macready's Benedick in 1888; and a description of Irving's 1882 production with Irving as Benedick, Ellen Terry as Beatrice, and Forbes Robertson as Claudio. For *Twelfth Night* Salgādo presents Charles Lamb's description of Dorothy Jordan's Olivia and Robert Bensley's Malvolio in 1814; a critique by Leigh Hunt of Kemble's production in 1811; descriptions of a Covent Garden production in 1820; a Sadler's Wells production in 1857; and a Lyceum production with Irving as Malvolio and Ellen Terry as Viola in 1884.

75. Speight, Robert. *Shakespeare on the Stage.* Boston: Little Brown, 1973.

Speight provides information about Harley Granville-Barker's important 1912 production of *Twelfth Night* at the Savoy Theatre. He offers descriptions, sometimes with illustrations, of two productions by Jacques Copeau—*Twelfth Night* at the Vieux Colombier in Paris in 1914 and *As You Like It* in Florence in 1938. He covers the production of *Much Ado*, directed by Gielgud, who also played Benedick, with Dorothy Tutin as Hero and Diana Wynyard as Beatrice in 1952; Gielgud's production of *Twelfth Night*, with Vivien Leigh as Viola and Laurence Olivier as Malvolio in 1955; and Peter Hall's RSC *Twelfth Night* of 1958.

76. Winter, William. *Shakespeare on the Stage.* Second Series. New York: Moffat, Yard, 1915.

Winter includes information about British and American productions in the eighteenth and nineteenth centuries for a selection of plays, including *As You Like It* and *Twelfth Night*; *Much Ado about Nothing* was scheduled for another volume, which was not completed. For *As You Like It*, Winter covers eighteenth-century productions beginning in 1740, including performances of Mrs. Siddons and Mrs. Jordan; sixty revivals on the nineteenth-century British stage with a long list of actresses who played Rosalind; productions on the American stage from 1786 to 1914 with lists of players of Rosalind, Touchstone, Jacques, and Orlando. For *Twelfth Night*, Winter covers Restoration revivals; Fleetwood's production of 1741; revivals from 1746 to 1825; Samuel Phelps's production at Sadler's Wells in 1848; Irving as Malvolio and Ellen Terry as Viola in 1884; Ellen Tree's Viola from 1863 to 1868; Adelaide Nielson's Viola in 1877; American productions from 1786 to 1914 with lists of players of Malvolio, Sir Toby, and Viola; Ada Rehan's Viola in 1914; Julia Marlowe as Viola in 1887 with E. H. Sothern as Malvolio; and Margaret Anglin as Viola from 1908 to 1914.

E. Pedagogy.

76a. **Cohen, Ralph Alan**, ed. *Shakespeare Quarterly* 41 (1990): 139–267.

This special issue of *Shakespeare Quarterly* is devoted to teaching and addresses the "upheaval" in Shakespeare criticism and how the variety of critical viewpoints may be translated into the classroom to destabilize any single approach or text. Marjorie Garber and Stephen Booth warn the reader against fetishizing Shakespeare. Several essays question the authority of the teacher in order to interrogate the discipline and shift the responsibility of dealing with a problematic Shakespeare to the collective effort of the students. Notable in the issue are Edward Rocklin's "'An Incarnational Art': Teaching Shakespeare" and Sharon A. Beehler's "'That's a Certain Text': Problematizing Shakespeare Instruction in American Schools and Colleges." *Shakespeare Quarterly* began devoting an issue to teaching under special editorship in 1974 and continued with another, largely devoted to teaching through performance, in 1984.

76b. **Cohen, Ralph Alan**, ed. *Shakespeare Quarterly* 46 (1995): 125–250.

This special issue, devoted to teaching at high school and college levels, is divided into three parts: "Viewpoint," "Methods," and "Tools." In the first section, Russ McDonald's "Shakespeare Goes to High School: Some Current Practices in the American Classroom," and Peggy O'Brien's "'And Gladly Teach': Books, Articles, and a Bibliography on the Teaching of Shakespeare" are helpful. In the second section, David Sauer's

"'Speak the speech, I pray you,' Or Suiting the Method to the Moment" and Milla Riggio's "The Universal is the Specific: Deviance and Cultural Identity in the Shakespeare Classroom" address current issues. In the third section, Martha Tuck Rozett's "Creating a Context for Shakespeare with Historical Fiction," Stephen Buhler's "Text, Eyes, and Videotape: Screening Shakespeare Scripts," and Michael J. Collins's "Using Films to Teach Shakespeare" have creative suggestions from their own practice.

76c. Cohen, Robert. *Acting in Shakespeare.* Mountain View, Calif.: Mayfield, 1991.

This is a handbook about how to teach students to perform Shakespeare using modern acting techniques. It discusses rhetorical formulas, costumes, physical movement, and the speaking of verse. It presents thirty-two roles, male and female, comic and tragic, as examples for approaching them. It also provides insights into passages used as exercises.

76d. Collins, Michael J. "Love, Sighs, and Videotape: An Approach to Teaching Shakespeare's Comedies." In *Teaching Shakespeare Today*, ed. James E. Davis and Ronald E. Salomone, 109–16. Urbana: National Council of Teachers of English, 1993.

Collins focuses on what the audience values in comedy—the joy of dreams come true—and he approaches Shakespeare's comedies through videotapes of modern comedies to help students define their reactions to familiar Hollywood films. In this way, the students grow to understand what is valuable about Shakespeare's comedies: "the complexity or ambiguity of feeling they evoke through their consistent refusal to rest easily in the conventions, particularly the conventional closure, of their own genre" (115).

76e. Grant, Cathy, ed. *As You Like It: Audiovisual Shakespeare.* London: British Universities Film and Video Council, 1992.

This is a reference work compiled by the British Shakespeare and Schools project (from the Shakespeare Institute of Education at Cambridge University). There is an introductory essay on teaching Shakespeare through video and film by Rex Gibson; David Olive writes about using video in teaching by performance; Raymond Ingram writes about aesthetic issues in the use of videos and the effects of filming scripts; and Murray Weston addresses copyright issues. The guide provides information about audio-visual versions of the plays and sonnets and background material for Shakespeare, most of it on video. Included is a bibliography. Although most of the materials are British, many items are available in the United States. For sources, see Rothwell and Melzer (no. 23).

77. **Leach, Susan.** "Race and Gender in Shakespeare," *Shakespeare in the Classroom*. Buckingham: Open Univ. Press, 1992.

Leach uses the comedies, with *Much Ado about Nothing* as a primary example, to show how conservative editing deprives students of a sense of how linguistically feisty Shakespeare's women are—even women like Hero. At the same time, she argues, students need to be made aware of how deeply patriarchal Shakespeare's texts are.

78. **McMurtry, Jo.** *Shakespeare Films in the Classroom*. Hamden: Archon Books, 1994.

This book provides listings of available films with casts, brief evaluations, textual cuts and rearrangements, settings, costumes, interpretations of roles, production history, reviews and studies, purchase and rental information. It contains information on three films of *As You Like It*, three of *Much Ado about Nothing*, and two of *Twelfth Night*.

See also no. 286.

F. Collections.

79. **Brown, J. R.,** and **Bernard Harris,** eds. *Shakespearian Comedy*. Stratford-upon-Avon Studies 14. London: Edward Arnold, 1972.

This collection contains essays by Anne Barton (no. 44), J. R. Brown, Inga-Stina Ewbank, Gareth Lloyd Evans (no. 31), R. A. Foakes, John Dixon Hunt, A. D. Nutall, D. J. Palmer, Jocelyn Powell, and Stanley Wells.

80. **Charney, Maurice,** ed. *Shakespearean Comedy*. New York: New York Literary Forum, 1980.

This volume has theoretical and interpretive essays by David Bergeron, William C. Carroll (no. 221), Maurice Charney, Louise George Clubb, Barbara Freedman, Elizabeth Freund, Marjorie Garber, Terence Hawkes, Harriet Hawkins, Malcolm Kiniry, Mary Ellen Lamb (no. 230), Ninian Mellamphy, Ruth Nevo, S. Georgia Nugent, Avraham Oz, Douglas L. Peterson, Jeanne A. Roberts, Leo Salingar, Catherine M. Shaw, Paul N. Siegel (no. 236), Susan Snyder, and Marion Trousdale.

81. **Muir, Kenneth,** ed. *Shakespeare: The Comedies, A Collection of Critical Essays*. Englewood Cliffs, N.J.: Prentice Hall, 1965.

Essays about early comedies, problem comedies, and romances are those by M. C. Bradbrook, Harold Brooks, R. W. Chambers, Bonamy

Dobree, G. W. Knight, Clifford Leech, J. Middleton Murry, Ernest Schanzer, and Derek Traversi. Those relevant to the middle comedies are the work of Helen Gardner on *As You Like It* (no. 120), of A. P. Rossiter on *Much Ado* (no. 189), and of Harold Jenkins on *Twelfth Night* (no. 261).

G. Bibliographies.

82. Champion, Larry S. *The Essential Shakespeare: An Annotated Bibliography of Major Modern Studies.* New York: G. K. Hall, 1986 (first edition), 1993 (second edition).

Champion's first edition covers modern scholarship to 1983; the second omits some items included in the first, expands the scope by 650 entries, and covers work through 1991. His criterion for inclusion is critical and scholarly significance. Both volumes list and annotate general studies, collected editions, biographies, criticism, dating and textual studies, source studies, background studies, works on language and style, stage and film history, thematic and topical studies. Champion offers a selection of books in general studies of each genre: histories, comedies, tragedies, romances, poems and sonnets; and a brief selection from article literature for each play. Because of deletions and additions, the reader is advised to consult both editions.

83. Kolin, Philip C. *Shakespeare and Feminist Criticism: An Annotated Bibliography and Commentary.* New York: Garland, 1991.

Kolin covers the feminist criticism of Shakespeare's plays and poems in books, dissertations, and articles from 1975 through 1988. His extended introduction covers a number of topics relevant to the middle comedies, such as dissolving gender boundaries, gender and theatrical representation, Shakespeare's androgynous heroines and the politics of gender, and gender and genre. His citations of 439 items are arranged chronologically, and the annotations are extensive and thorough.

84. Mahood, M. M. "Shakespeare's Middle Comedies: A Generation of Criticism," *Shakespeare Survey* 32 (1979), 1–13.

In this comprehensive review essay, Mahood summarizes and evaluates criticism of *As You Like It, Much Ado about Nothing,* and *Twelfth Night* from 1950 to 1975 in British and American journals and monographs. She explores the changing fashions in criticism, in addition to grouping scholarship around topics such as the "green world," the language of the plays, and the fool.

85. Sajdak, Bruce. *Shakespeare Index: An Annotated Bibliography of Critical Articles on the Plays 1959–1983.* 2 vols. Millwood, N.Y.: Kraus International Publications, 1992. Vol. 1, Citations and Author Index. Vol. 2, Character, Scene, and Subject Indexes.

Sajdak seeks to provide the student with a means to "quickly locate, amongst the thousands of possible sources, those few most relevant articles on specific ideas, characters, or scenes" (xi). His readers are those "who wish to study critical or background articles on *specific* aspects of the plays" (xi). He provides a statement of scope so that the reader can quickly discover what is excluded from the work, a list of sources he consulted (xiii–xvii), and a guide on how to use the *Index* (xxi–xxii). Sajdak divides the *Index* into 48 chapters (each arranged chronologically by date of publication), initially by research area (for instance, political, economic, social, and cultural backgrounds); and theme, character, and other general studies; then by play title, arranged by period, genre, and title. For each entry, Sajdak provides full publication information and an annotation; he covers 7,116 articles.

86. Smallwood, R. L. "The Middle Comedies." In *Shakespeare: A Bibliographical Guide*, new edition, ed. Stanley Wells. Oxford: Clarendon, 1990.

Smallwood includes *The Merchant of Venice* and *The Merry Wives of Windsor* in the middle comedies. He presents an essay before a selected bibliography of about 200 items from 1970 to 1989. Works included are editions and scholarly studies, criticism and commentary, and studies of the plays in performance.

III. AS YOU LIKE IT

A. Editions.

87. Brissenden, Alan, ed. *As You Like It*. Oxford: Clarendon Press, 1993.

The text is based on the Folio of 1623, modernized following Wells's principles for the Oxford Shakespeare. The extensive introduction covers dating (1599–1600); sources and a comparison of the play with a narrative summary of Thomas Lodge's *Rosalynde*; love and metamorphosis; doubleness, that is, role-playing and pairs of characters; names and places; pastoral; the play in performance illustrated; and "your very, very Rosalind," a running account of the part. The editor acknowledges recent commentary on cross-dressing, boy-actors, and Rosalind as "the greatest of Shakespeare's comic heroines" (56). Appendix A addresses the contemporary, especially bawdy, meanings of *wit*. Appendix B presents musical settings for the songs. The notes at the bottom of the page compare the play to Lodge's narrative; set the scenes; give readings of metaphors and other rhetorical figures; provide glosses, especially the many bawdy glosses; and explain allusions.

88. Hattaway, Michael, ed. *As You Like It*. The New Cambridge Shakespeare. Cambridge: Cambridge Univ. Press, 2000.

The text is the First Folio, with emendations rationalized in a "Note on the Text" (67) and "Textual Analysis" (199–203). Hattaway presents a detailed introduction that deals with the settings, the place of the play in comedic genres, the pastoral and counter-pastoral element, the "condition of the country," contemporary politics, sexuality and gender, nuptials, stage history (illustrated), screen history, dating and original occasion (1599–1600), and a brief description of the sources. Appendix 1 provides substantial extracts from the principal source, Thomas Lodge's *Rosalynde*. Appendix 2 provides references for the five songs of the play. There is also a brief reading list. Notes at the bottom of the page set scenes, provide ample glosses, explain allusions (with references), and provide stage directions. Notes are provided to the characters' names. The introduction is the best now available and very well annotated.

89. Knowles, Richard, ed. *A New Variorum Edition of Shakespeare: "As You Like It"* with a Survey of Criticism by Evelyn Joseph Mattern. New York: Modern Language Association of America, 1977.

The text is a modified reprint of the First Folio, correcting errors and retaining lineation. Knowles presents line-by-line commentary; discussion of the text; and dating the play (1598–1600). About sources Knowles offers the text of *Rosalynde* with comments on Shakespeare's use of Lodge; a synopsis of *Gamelyn*; information about ballads and folklore sources for Robin Hood; commentary on the stage pastoral; discussion of the influence of Lyly, Sidney, Greene, and other English contemporaries, as well as classical and continental sources. Summaries of critical commentary cover two centuries from 1765 to 1972 and are extensive for eighteenth- and nineteenth-century criticism. Knowles includes stage history; "The Text on the Stage," a description of what was cut for eighteenth- and nineteenth-century performances; and a discussion of the songs.

90. Latham, Agnes, ed. *As You Like It*. Arden Edition of the Works of William Shakespeare. London: Methuen, 1975.

The text is based on First Folio with modernized spelling and stage directions. A substantial introduction (ix–xci) deals with the text, including copy, acts and scenes, stage directions, punctuation and variants, verse and prose, the masque, and songs; date of composition (1599), including verse fossils; the time scheme; the relative height of Rosalind and Celia; sources, including a comparison to Lodge's *Rosalynde*, Jacques and contemporary satirists, the country clowns, Lyly and the "love-cure," and pastoral names; people and themes with character analyses and readings of set speeches. A stage history is also included. Latham's notes at the bottom of the page provide glosses, explain puns and allusions, and give references where disputes among scholars arise.

B. Date and Text.

For a thorough discussion of the date of *As You Like It*, see Knowles (no. 89). Claims that *As You Like It* is *Love's Labour's Won*, listed among Shakespeare's plays by Francis Meres in *Palladis Tamia* (1598), have implications for the date of *As You Like It* because the title is not listed by Meres, and the play is usually dated somewhat later than 1598. For the latest claim, see Wickham (no. 144); for a summary of the arguments, pro and con, see Knowles (no. 89). Knowles and Latham (no. 90) are the best editions to consult about the text of the play.

C. Influences; Sources; Historical and Intellectual Backgrounds; Topicality.

91. Bennett, Robert B. "The Reform of a Malcontent: Jacques and the Meaning of *As You Like It.*" *Shakespeare Studies* 9 (1976): 183–204.

Bennett examines Jacques in the context of a collection of Elizabethan malcontents, Hamlet, Malevole in John Marston's *The Malcontent*, Bussy D'Ambois in George Chapman's *Bussy D'Ambois*, Vindice in Cyril Tourneur's *The Revenger's Tragedy*, Flamineo in John Webster's *The White Devil*, and Bosola in Webster's *The Duchess of Malfi*. They are characters with unfulfilled talents, intelligence, energy, and ability. For Bennett, "The multi-sided and high-spirited intellect is the malcontent's most significant dramatic characteristic" (185). Bennett points out that Jacques is Elizabethan drama's only fully developed comic malcontent, and thus the play depicts the process whereby Jacques is gradually cleansed of his malaise. By the end he has abandoned melancholy and cynicism and has replaced rancor with measured opinions. For Bennett, Jacques's judgments of the other characters are apt and his choice of the contemplative life a positive one.

92. Berry, Edward I. "Rosalynde and Rosalind." *Shakespeare Quarterly* 31(1980): 42–52. Repr. in Bloom (no. 149).

Berry compares Rosalynde in Lodge's *Rosalynde* to Shakespeare's character, demonstrating how Shakespeare creates complexity while following closely the outlines of Lodge's heroine. The essay explores, especially, the psychological implications for Rosalind in the Silvius-Phebe episodes and defines clearly the stages of Rosalind's development. This is the most subtle study of a much studied heroine.

93. Cirillo, Albert R. "*As You Like It*: Pastoralism Gone Awry." *ELH* 38 (1971): 19–39. Repr. in Scott (no. 151).

Cirillo continues the debate about the meaning of the pastoral in *As You Like It*. Shakespeare, Cirillo argues, seeks "to make the pastoral a necessarily ephemeral but educative experience for the characters in the comedy....[B]y consistently undercutting the pastoral convention *as a convention*, he also suggests that the ideal of the pastoral is not an end in itself...but the underlying substance of the real, the world of the possible which should inform the actual" (19). For Cirillo, the Forest is a magic circle, a testing ground for love, a curative place for Oliver and Frederick, but, in his view, the pastoral must be recognized as artifice to become "a genuine view of truth" (33).

94. Dusinberre, Juliet. "As *Who* Liked It?" *Shakespeare Survey* 46 (1994): 9–21.

Dusinberre connects *As You Like It* to Elizabeth I, to John Harington, translator of *Orlando Furioso*, and to Rabelais. While some of the connections may seem strained, the insistence that "*As You Like It* seems to me to rewrite the record of female desire so that women want to read it," is well taken, as are the general connections to Rabelais and the link of Rosalind to Elizabeth I. Dusinberre believes that Rabelais's motto *Fay ce que voudras* is "a message for women rather than for men, at least in Shakespeare's time," (21) because, Dusinberre says, "as you like it" meant as men liked it, except as fantasy in the theatre.

95. Erickson, Peter. *Patriarchal Structures in Shakespeare's Drama.* Berkeley: Univ. of California Press, 1985. Selection repr. in Scott (no. 151).

Erickson replies to feminists and other critics who emphasize Rosalind's androgynous roles, her wit, and her control of the action. He argues that, far from being powerful at the end of the play, Rosalind accedes to patriarchal marriage in which she passes from father to husband in submission to prevailing social structures. Erickson also stresses the way that men gain power in this play through sustaining a strong male community and through assimilating female qualities of compassion and nurturing. See Montrose (no. 103), for similar arguments from a new historicist perspective.

96. Hieatt, Charles W. "The Quality of Pastoral in *As You Like It.*" *Genre* 7 (1974): 164–82.

Hieatt attempts to locate as precisely as possible how *As You Like It* fits into the Renaissance pastoral tradition. He sorts out the differences between pastoral drama and pastoral romance. For him, the comedy is a pastoral romance, as reflected in its tripartite structure and its importation of characters from a variety of classes and literary genres. Hieatt argues that the presence of Corin and Jacques in Arden allows Shakespeare to call ideals into question without destroying them and that Silvius and Phebe exceed the pastoral roles assigned to them, but revert to generic demands at the end.

97. Howard, Jean E. "Crossdressing, the Theatre, and Gender Struggle in Early Modern England." *Shakespeare Quarterly* 39 (1988): 418–40.

In this wide-ranging essay, Howard questions whether female crossdressing on the stage is a site of resistance to the patriarchal system, when crossdressing often stresses what the disguised woman cannot do. For

Howard, Rosalind's role is complex because while costumed as a boy, she plays the Petrarchan beloved, making the audience aware of the construction of the feminine in that discourse. In Howard's reading, the role of the boy actor in the epilogue—still in drag—continues the destabilization of gender identities, just as all the characters—or nearly all—have reassumed their former social positions at the play's end. For further comments on gender and crossdressing, see also Orgel (no. 35), Shapiro (no. 36), and Rackin (no. 60).

98. Knowles, Richard. "Myth and Type in *As You Like It*." *ELH* 33 (1966): 1–22.

Knowles explores the classical references in *As You Like It*, particularly those relating Orlando to Hercules, and he also addresses the more interesting question of the effect of allusions in the play. He concludes, "The education in love and self-knowledge that Orlando sought at the beginning of the play and has been receiving from Duke Senior and Rosalind is finally completed with his Herculean defeat of self-love (arrogance and envy) and his charitable rescue of his sinful brother" (20).

99. Kott, Jan. "The Gender of Rosalind." *New Theatre Quarterly* 7 (1991): 113–25.

Kott connects the androgynous effects of Rosalind/Ganymede with a moment in French history (the mid–1830's) when life and literature were obsessed "with the theme of the androgyne—aesthetic, erotic, and social" (121). This preoccupation was especially notable for George Sand, Gautier, Merimee, Balzac, and de Musset. Thus Kott emphasizes the importance for cultural history of Rosalind's androgyny. See a reply in Soule (no. 106).

100. Kronenfeld, Judy Z. "Social Rank and the Pastoral Ideals of *As You Like It*." *Shakespeare Quarterly* 29 (1978): 333–48.

For Kronenfeld, *As You Like It* is a contrast to most Renaissance pastoral works, which reaffirm the social hierarchy by giving the noble shepherd a monopoly on virtue. Here, according to Kronenfeld, Corin and Adam are genuine examples of pastoral virtue, even if Audrey and William are dolts; Orlando makes his nobility evident by noble deeds, while Touchstone reminds us of the limitations of gentility. "Shakespeare, working within the tradition, does not really 'unmask' the pastoral; he merely puts pressure on its social vision in order to revivify it" (348). According to Kronenfeld, the virtues of the highborn are reaffirmed through deed. For additional socio-economic readings, see Krieger (no. 55), Montrose (no. 103), and Wilson (no. 109).

101. McFarland, Thomas. *Shakespeare's Pastoral Comedy.* Chapel Hill: Univ. of North Carolina Press, 1972.

McFarland analyzes Shakespeare's complications of the pastoral tradition in *As You Like It*, which, he says, begins with usurpation, banishment, and brother-brother rivalries. McFarland accents the bleak side of the comedy, which is redeemed by what goes on in the forest. "The comic reclamation in the Forest of Arden involves complicated character interactions and severe criticisms of behavior" (99). For McFarland, *As You Like It* makes a "massive assault of the forces of bitterness and alienation upon the pastoral vision of Shakespeare, and its action glances off the dark borders of tragedy" (101).

102. Mincoff, Marco. "What Shakespeare Did to *Rosalynd*." *Shakespeare Jahrbuch* 96 (1960): 78-89. Selection repr. in Halio (no. 150).

Mincoff argues that what Shakespeare takes from Lodge is not an "inquiry into the pastoral," but the theme of love's foolishness and the discrepancies between appearance and reality. He sketches Shakespeare's profound debt to Lodge, despite structural rearrangements necessary to transmute a novel into a play. Mincoff says Shakespeare's greatest debt is the character of Rosalind, whose complexity may be greater in Lodge, but whose wonderful language is Shakespeare's. For further comments on Rosalind, see Berry (no. 92) and Bloom (no. 149).

103. Montrose, Louis A. " 'The Place of a Brother' in *As You Like It*: Social Process and Comic Form." *Shakespeare Quarterly* 32 (1981): 28-54. Selection repr. in Scott (no. 151).

In a new historicist essay, Montrose shows how the comic form with its ending in marriage resolves the social predicament of the younger son, Orlando, in a system of primogeniture. "Shakespeare uses the machinery of pastoral romance to remedy the lack of fit between deserving and having, between Nature and Fortune" (33). Rosalind's energetic control of the wooing and wedding is contained, according to Montrose, by the social subordination of woman to both father and husband, and the fraternity of all males in cuckoldry defends against the threat men feel from women. This essay has become highly influential. For contrasting views of cuckoldry, see Williamson (no. 38), Cook (no. 178), and Fineman (no. 251).

104. Palmer, D. J. "Art and Nature in *As You Like It*." *Philological Quarterly* 49 (1970): 30-40. Repr. in Scott (no. 151).

Palmer answers Barber (no. 28), and Jenkins (no. 123), who stress the contrasts and the antitheses in the play, by showing how Art and Nature, the controlling ideas of the pastoral genre, extend one another. Nature is discovered through Art, which is itself of Nature's making. Palmer shows how Art and Nature work through Duke Senior's reaction to Arden, through Oliver's conversion, through Touchstone's artful parodies, and through Rosalind's feigning, to come to natural truth. He concludes, "The Forest of Arden represents Nature as Art, not only when we accept it as an unreal pastoral world, but equally in its properties as a teacher and as a restorer of Nature's equilibrium. For those who enter there, and encounter each other under its auspices, are cast by reflection into their natural roles." (40)

105. Scoufos, Alice-Lyle. "The *Paradiso Terrestre* and the Testing of Love in *As You Like It*." *Shakespeare Studies* 14 (1981): 215–27. Selection repr. in Scott (no. 151).

Scoufos focuses on the conventions of the earthly paradise and the testing of the levels of love, according to the Neoplatonic ladder. She connects the action and details of the play to the Neoplatonic system. In Scoufos's reading, Orlando passes three tests: the first is the transformation of violence into gentleness, with which he learns to treat the Duke and his followers; the second is faith to the ideal of Rosalind, despite the taunts of Ganymede; and the third is loving his evil brother when sorely tempted to leave Oliver to the lioness. For Neoplatonism and *Much Ado*, see Lewalski (no. 163).

106. Soule, Lesley Anne. "Subverting Rosalind: Cocky Ros in the Forest of Arden." *New Theatre Quarterly* 7 (1991): 126–36.

Soule argues that Rosalind is far from the ideal female critics and directors have made her, but a composite figure in which two identities counterpoint one another. For Soule, it is therefore important to see Ganymede as Cocky Roscius, whose lineage is the vice figure, who mocks his betters and shares qualities of both sexes as well as adolescent and adult characteristics. "His presence thus provides the means to contrast a distant, high-status, verse-speaking, fictional, appropriable Rosalind with a foregrounded, lower-status, popular language-speaking, physical, inappropriable stage actor" (135). For an androgynous Rosalind, see Kott (no. 99).

107. Traci, Philip. "*As You Like It*: Homosexuality in Shakespeare's Play." *College Language Association Journal* 25 (1981): 91–105.

Traci claims that Shakespeare actively explores the homosexuality of the actors playing Rosalind/Ganymede and Orlando. He supports his argument with historical evidence of homosexuality among the boy actors and suggests that the original audience might have known of the relationships among the players. Traci asserts that the epilogue and other scenes also deal with alternative sexualities. This is one of the earliest articles about what has become a major theme of recent criticism of the play; see, for example, Shapiro (no. 36), Traub (no. 62), Wofford (no. 114), and Pequigney (no. 265).

108. Williamson, Marilyn L. "The Masque of Hymen in *As You Like It*." *Comparative Drama* 2 (1968-9): 248-58.

Williamson asserts that the Masque of Hymen is not a tacked-on afterthought, unrelated to the rest of the play, and argues instead that the masque shows Shakespeare using the full resources of the pastoral mode, which frequently mixes allegorical characters with real-life figures, like Corin. According to Williamson, the masque invites a distant perspective on the characters, who lose individuality and become creatures whose immortality in progeny "peoples every town" (5.4.142); and as the characters head for the Ark, seeing them as part of a species offers a renewal that answers the effects of devouring Time.

109. Wilson, Richard. "'Like the old Robin Hood': *As You Like It* and the Enclosure Riots." *Shakespeare Quarterly* 43 (1992): 1-19.

Wilson claims that the subsistence crisis of the 1590s is urgently represented in *As You Like It*: "No Shakespearean text transmits more urgently the imminence of the social breakdown threatened by the conjuncture of famine and enclosure" (3-4). Orlando speaks for the masterless men; like Robin Hood, he becomes a social bandit. Wilson sees Oliver's story as "the rise of gentry by engrossing and enclosure" (5). For this critic, Rosalind and Celia act roles of the "shemale" and "black" in contemporary peasant rebellions. But in the end, Wilson argues, the marriage of Rosalind and Orlando affirms the appropriation of popular laughter by the gentility and nobility, a "paradigm of the state's appropriation of English Carnival" (19).

110. Young, David. *The Heart's Forest: A Study of Shakespeare's Pastoral Plays*. New Haven: Yale Univ. Press, 1972. Selection repr. in Scott (no. 151).

Young attempts to treat the pastoral as an Elizabethan convention and at the same time deal with its use in a variety of Shakespeare's plays: *As You Like It, King Lear, Winter's Tale,* and *Tempest*. Young emphasizes the artificiality of the pastoral in *As You Like It* and explains how the play exploits the contingent "if" to display that quality. For Young, the forest becomes a mirror that reflects individual characters, and all characters display highly variable traits. "In *As You Like It* we are invited to view the pastoral convention simultaneously from the inside, as in Lodge, and from the outside, as a frankly artificial and illusory construction" (70).

D. Language and Linguistics.

111. Crane, Mary Thomas. "Linguistic Change, Theatrical Practice, and the Ideologies of Status in *As You Like It*." *English Literary Renaissance* 27 (1997): 361–92.

Crane argues that *As You Like It* uses language to call attention to potentially disruptive ideas about upward social mobility, while at the same time imperfectly managing these elements through two techniques. First, characters shift class referents to gradations of status within the 'gentle' classes; and, second, they use classical allusions that distance or neutralize social distinctions. According to Crane, these effects are reinforced by a possible shift from Will Kemp playing the Fool more broadly with his jigs to Robert Armin, who played a more subtle and refined Fool. Crane contends that, through the use of status terms as "villain" and "clown," through representation on stage of the concerns of dispossessed laborers and servants, and through assimilation of jig motifs into the play itself, *As You Like It* qualifies its own implication in the social mechanisms that made possible limited upward mobility for a few based on the exclusion of others. For comments on the change from Kemp to Armin in Shakespeare's company, see Evans (no. 31).

112. Lifson, Martha K. "Learning by Talking: Conversation in *As You Like It*." *Shakespeare Survey* 40 (1988): 91–105.

Lifson uses rhetorical and psychoanalytic concepts to discuss what Orlando and Rosalind teach one another in the Forest. "The self-knowledge they both come to is dependent on their acceding to deceitfulness as a concept and a mode of behavior" (94). For Lifson, language is used both to display and to conceal sexual desire, and Hymen's appearance at the end is a visible manifestation of the lovers' choosing to extend the pretence of Arden into belief within the ordinary world. "This play educates its characters and its audience in the value of 'if' " (105). Lifson and Ronk (no. 113) are the same author.

113. Ronk, Martha. "Locating the Visual in *As You Like It*." *Shakespeare Quarterly* 52 (2001): 255–76.

Ronk focuses on the relation between the verbal and the visual in the play. "Shakespeare purposely draws attention to the ways in which the one aspect of the theater plays against the other such that what is presented is layered and qualified" (255). She stresses the frictions between the staging and ekphrasis (pictures in words) and between sight and speech. Ronk uses Orlando's bad poems about Rosalind as examples of the failure to represent the character in words, just as Rosalind's own descriptions of herself do not represent her complexity. For Ronk, the pastoral presents nature in a paradoxical artificiality. Ronk concludes, "*As You Like It* carries a theory of theatrical production within it—as it insistently enacts disruption and the various ways in which any character, scene, or abstract idea might be represented" (274). Ronk and Lifson (no. 112) are the same author.

114. Wofford, Susanne. "'To You I Give Myself, For I Am Yours': Erotic Performance and Theatrical Performatives in *As You Like It*." In *Shakespeare Reread: The Texts in New Contexts*, ed. Russ McDonald, 147-69. Ithaca, N.Y.: Cornell Univ. Press, 1994.

Wofford explores the use of proxy identities and performative language to accomplish deeds that will forestall threats to the happy ending. She claims that the homoerotic subtexts of the wooing do not threaten the marriage system, which preserves male-male bonds and breaks those between women, and the wooing wards off the threat of the unruly woman. Wofford explains how the repetition of ritual gestures, such as the double marriage, serves to contain the socially innovative gesture—Rosalind's giving herself in marriage, for example.

See also nos. 39-41, 140.

E. Criticism.

115. Barnet, Sylvan. "'Strange Events': Improbability in *As You Like It*." *Shakespeare Studies* 4 (1968): 119-31. Repr. in Scott (no. 151).

Barnet argues that Shakespeare exaggerates the improbabilities of *As You Like It*. Barnet claims that Shakespeare removes clear motivations described in *Rosalynde*, makes the love affairs instantaneous, makes the villains suffer sudden conversions, and makes Hymen appear mysteriously at the end. For Barnet, the characters engage in strange behavior "because strange behavior is what Shakespeare is talking about" (129).

116. Beckman, Margaret B. "The Figure of Rosalind in *As You Like It*." *Shakespeare Quarterly* 29 (1978): 44-51.

Beckman presents *As You Like It* as a work that reconciles opposites.

It shows the audience pairs of concepts and perspectives "in which both members of the opposition are retained in the face of all temptation to choose one or the other" (46). For Beckman, the central representative of this harmony is Rosalind, who balances idealism and realism, male and female, wit and compassion; and, Beckman claims, the play itself constantly balances freedom and limits, melancholy and laughter, humble and high estate, court and country life, danger and safety, time and timelessness, without one of any opposition deposing the other. For a similar interpretation, see Jenkins (no. 123).

117. Berry, Ralph. "No Exit from Arden." *Modern Language Review* 66 (1971): 11–20.

Berry studies the power relationships in *As You Like It* in great detail. He finds that the drive to control another human being "is the underlying theme of much of the dialogue" (11). Oliver cannot bear the shadow of Orlando, Frederick hates his brother, Jacques resents Duke Senior, and Rosalind "is motivated above all by a will to dominate" (15). Finally, Touchstone "is the reduction of the ideas latent in *As You Like It*. He exhibits in gross form the will to mastery that is discernible in the actions of his betters" (19).

118. Carroll, William C. "Forget to Be a Woman." In *The Metamorphoses of Shakespearean Comedy*, 127–37. Princeton: Princeton Univ. Press, 1985. Repr. in Bloom (no. 149).

Carroll deals with Rosalind as the center of a circle of real and apparent transformations. He argues that the ability to feign allows Rosalind to transform herself effectively, but that other transformations, those of Oliver and Duke Frederick, are apparently caused by the Forest and seem strained. The play takes seriously transformations through the power of love, according to Carroll, and the change of Rosalind into Ganymede is more complex than the sex changes in the other comedies because it allows him/her to ridicule both sexes and their stereotypes simultaneously. For Carroll, after Hymen replaces Rosalind as the chief engineer of the action, the final metamorphosis of she into he takes place in the Epilogue.

119. Garber, Marjorie. "The Education of Orlando." In *Comedy from Shakespeare to Sheridan: Change and Continuity in the English and European Dramatic Tradition*, ed. A. R. Braunmuller and J. C. Bulman, 102–12. Newark: Univ. of Delaware Press, 1986.

Garber argues that Rosalind chooses to stay, unnecessarily, disguised as Ganymede in order to educate Orlando in the ways of love and about herself; she brings him from a tongue-tied victim of love at first sight to one who declares "I can live no longer by thinking" (5.2.49). For Garber, the long process of wooing contrasts with the suddenness of the conversion of Oliver and his wooing of Celia, whose mating acts as a catalyst for Orlando. According to Garber, although he may never be the equal of Rosalind, Orlando comes a long way.

120. Gardner, Helen. "*As You Like It.*" In *More Talking of Shakespeare*, ed. John Garrett, 17–32. London: Longmans, Green, 1959. Repr. in Muir (no. 81), Halio (no. 150), and Scott (no. 151).

Gardner echoes some of the points made by Jenkins (no. 123), but adds her own comments about the discovery of truth through lies and feigning. She stresses the presence of Jacques as the one character who questions the completeness of the comic vision. She shows that the lessons learned in Arden are bitter, though not so bitter as those in Lear's place of exile. While she does not mention those who choose to remain in Arden, Gardner says the exiles are happy to leave.

121. Goldsmith, Robert H. *Wise Fools in Shakespeare*. East Lansing: Michigan State Univ. Press, 1955.

Goldsmith perceives a change in Touchstone from a simple fool in Act 1 to a wise fool in Act 5. Yet, Goldsmith argues, Touchstone is unlike Feste in never dwelling on his own wisdom: his parodies include self-mockery. And he is unlike Jacques in remaining detached and in exposing the absurdity of the melancholy wise person. For another perspective on Touchstone, see Wilcher (no. 65).

122. Halio, Jay L. "'No Clock in the Forest': Time in *As You Like It*," *Studies in English Literature 1500–1900* 2 (1962): 197–207. Selections repr. in Halio (no. 150) and Scott (no. 151).

Halio argues that the timelessness of the Forest links life in Arden with the ideal of an antique way of life that helps regenerate a corrupt present. According to Halio, Shakespeare balances the various perceptions of time: the natural process of ripening and rotting, the seven stages of man, the perception of individuals depending on their situations. These varied perspectives show that "neither the extremes of idealism nor those of materialism ... emerge as 'the good life' in *As You Like It*" (207).

123. Jenkins, Harold. "*As You Like It.*" *Shakespeare Survey* 8 (1955): 40–51. Selections repr. in Halio (no. 150) and Scott (no. 151).

Jenkins observes emphatically that nothing much happens in *As You Like It*, but, for him, this is less a defect than an omission to make way for "the art of comic juxtaposition ... at its subtlest" (43): although life in the Forest is an idealized contrast to the court, Shakespeare presents criticism of Arden at its very center from Touchstone, Jacques, and Corin. For Jenkins, this balance of criticism and idealism is the mark of Shakespeare's mature comedic practice; as the couples come and go, "Every view of life that is presented seems, sooner or later, to find its opposite" (50); even Rosalind has "the sanity to recognize that 'love is merely a madness'" (50). Throughout the play, Jenkins claims, ideals are mocked, but cherished. This essay is one of the first to stress the balance of perspectives and opposites in the play. For a development of this idea, see Beckman (no. 116).

124. Kerrigan, William. "Female Friends and Fraternal Enemies in *As You Like It*." In *Desire in the Renaissance: Psychoanalysis and Literature*, ed. Valeria Finucci and Regina Schwartz, 184–203. Princeton: Princeton Univ. Press, 1994.

Kerrigan demonstrates how *As You Like It* forestalls the onslaught of the hate-theme in the tragedies by emphasizing the resolution of sibling rivalry in both genders: Rosalind and Celia, Oliver and Orlando, Duke Senior and Frederick. And the play elaborately resolves, he argues as well, the fear of the mother. The epilogue, which exposes the entire absence of women in the cast, shows for Kerrigan "to the limits of Shakespeare's imagination that men can reconfigure their dread of women" (199).

125. Marshall, Cynthia. "The Doubled Jacques and Constructions of Negation in *As You Like It*." *Shakespeare Quarterly* 49 (1998): 375–92.

Marshall combines a Lacanian reading of the play with the observation that the two Jacques may not be a careless error. Instead, she claims that "Jacques serves as a kind of placeholder, standing in for the missing brother, Jacques de Boys, but also, more importantly, standing in for acknowledgement of loss and sadness in Arden's merry crew. He functions, that is, to forestall the threat of melancholia, but in (successfully) doing so, he also figures melancholia's threatening estrangement of self from self." (377) Marshall argues that, even more than Rosalind's Ganymede, Jacques "exemplifies the power of a symbol [as in Freud's *Fort/da*] to hold at bay a repressed and troubling idea" (383). The article explores the relation of melancholy to maternal loss, and to the many losses of freedom in marriage, defined by Hymen's rigid gender oppositions: "The melancholy Jacques has helped keep gender questions open; more broadly he has allowed the opening up of discourse, an enriched thinking" (391).

126. Swinden, Patrick. *An Introduction to Shakespeare's Comedies*. New

York: Barnes & Noble, 1973. Selections repr. in Scott (no. 151).

Swinden believes that *As You Like It* is "the most perfect of Shakespeare's comedies" (110). He notes that the plot is almost nonexistent, that the play develops by bringing characters together for dispute and argument. He sees the prominence of Rosalind's role as another difference from earlier comedies: "With the certainty about love that is guaranteed in Rosalind's person comes a new and comprehensive facility with wit and an astringency that consorts well with the endorsement of sentiment at the heart of the play" (117). Swinden analyses the way in which Rosalind plays off Jacques and Touchstone to achieve these effects.

F. Stage History and Performance Criticism.

127. Bowe, John. "Orlando in *As You Like It.*" In *Players of Shakespeare: Essays in Shakespearean Performance by Twelve Players with the Royal Shakespeare Company*, ed. Philip Brockbank, 67–76. Cambridge: Cambridge Univ. Press, 1985.

Bowe discusses the challenge of playing Orlando in the RSC production of 1980, not the least of which was getting injured in the wrestling match. He gives ample detail about the development of the games with Rosalind/Ganymede.

128. Bulman, J. C. "*As You Like It* and the Perils of Pastoral." In *Shakespeare on Television: An Anthology of Essays and Reviews*, ed. J. C. Bulman and H. R. Coursen, 174–79. Hanover: Univ. Press of New England, 1988. Repr. in Tomarken (no. 152).

Bulman explores Basil Coleman's solution to Cedric Messina's decision to locate filming of *As You Like It* in the surroundings of Glamis Castle. "Taking his cue from satirical qualifications of the pastoral in the play, he [Coleman] apparently decided that no television audience could swallow pastoral artifices straight, especially when they are played out in a location that by tradition demands realism. Thus he chose to alienate us from the fiction, to make the retreat to Arden seem a game that the players play only to keep from acknowledging the darker lessons that Jacques insists on." (179) The essay explores in detail Ganymede's femininity, the masque of Hymen, and Jacques's melancholy vision. This volume also contains excerpts from reviews of television productions from 1949 to 1985.

129. Crowl, Samuel. "Free Style." In *Shakespeare Observed: Studies in Performance on Stage and Screen*, 122–41. Athens: Ohio Univ. Press, 1992.

Crowl writes in detail about Adrian Noble's productions of *King Lear* and *As You Like It* by the Royal Shakespeare Company in 1985. He observes that the comedy is set in the post-World War I period and displays elegance in costumes and stage furniture. Crowl is full of praise for the actors' performances and for the conception of Arden as a state of mind, rather than a material place. The essay sympathetically evokes a major production of the play.

130. Derrick, Patty S. "Rosalind and the Nineteenth-Century Woman: Four Stage Interpretations." *Theatre Survey* 26 (1985): 143-62.

Derrick describes in detail the performances of four important nineteenth-century actresses interpreting Rosalind: Helen Modjeska in 1882-87, Mary Anderson in 1885-89, Ada Rehan in 1889, and Julia Marlowe in 1890.

131. Dessen, Alan C. "Problems and Options in *As You Like It.*" *Shakespeare Bulletin* 8 (1990): 18-21.

Dessen reviews five productions: a student presentation at Sewanee; the 1983 Stratford, Ontario, production on tape; an ACTER production of 1990; the 1990 production at Stratford, Ontario; and the 1989-90 RSC production. "What stood out for me after seeing this array of shows ... was not any single actor or actress but rather the range of approaches to recurring problems, many of them elusive to a reader, a playgoer, or even a theatrical professional" (18).

132. Hamer, Mary. "Shakespeare's Rosalind and Her Public Image." *Theatre Research International* 11 (1986): 105-18.

On the occasion of Juliet Stevenson's playing Rosalind in Adrian Noble's *As You Like It* in 1985, Hamer observes that the role of Rosalind is perceived by the public as a special challenge, a perception intensified by the stunning success of Vanessa Redgrave in the 1961 production. Hamer explains this assumption about the play and the role by a review of eighteenth- and nineteenth-century productions: "In the course of two centuries, as the play from 1741 onwards became ever more firmly established in the popular taste, the presentation of its heroine became fixed in a predictably idealizing mode" (107). She notes that tragic actresses avoided the role, and in the twentieth century only Edith Evans brought an intellectual edge to the part. Hamer concludes that *As You Like It* does not deserve its reputation: "I do not think that Juliet Stevenson necessarily failed. Rather she confirmed my long-held suspicion that the charm of Rosalind and the wonder of Arden do not stand up to scrutiny—feel their power you have to ... want very much to be enchanted" (117). For a collection of essays praising Rosalind, see Bloom (no. 149).

133. Jamieson, Michael. "*As You Like It*—Performance and Reception." In *"As You Like It"—from 1660 to the Present*, ed. Edward Tomarken, 623-46. New York: Garland, 1997.

Jamieson traces the history of performances from the 1740 London production to the 1995 Cheek by Jowl production in London. In this account Jamieson remarks on famous Rosalinds, such as Dora Jordan from 1787 to 1814, the American Charlotte Cushman from 1845 to 1857, Dame Edith Evans in 1936, Peggy Ashcroft from 1951 to 1957, Vanessa Redgrave in 1961, and Maggie Smith from 1977 to 1979. Productions that merit extended comment are Macready's at Drury Lane in 1842 with Helena Faucit as Rosalind; Lady Archibald Campbell's Aesthetic production of 1884-85; Nigel Playfair's production of 1919 at the Memorial Theatre; Jules Supervielle's at the Theatre des Champs-Elysees in Paris and Jacques Copeau's at the Theatre de L'Atelier, both in 1934; *Rosalinda* in Rome staged by Luchino Visconti in 1948; an American version with Katharine Hepburn in 1950; three productions of Byam Shaw in the 1950s; the 1961 Royal Shakespeare Company production; the all-male production at the National Theatre in 1967-71; a Regency version with Maggie Smith at Stratford, Ontario, in 1977-78; Peter Stein's radical production at the Schaubühne in West Berlin in 1979; John Dexter's at the National Theatre in 1979; and two much-traveled productions of Cheek by Jowl between 1991 and 1995.

134. Kennedy, Dennis. "Well, this is the Forest of Arden." In *Looking at Shakespeare: A Visual History of Twentieth-Century Performance*, 257-65. Cambridge: Cambridge Univ. Press, 1993.

This well-illustrated essay covers four productions of *As You Like It*. Kennedy reports that Clifford Williams's all-male production for the National Theatre at the Old Vic created a sensation in 1967; and although the production did not have the intended effect of conveying a love that transcends sexuality, the absence of women renewed interest on the part of critics and directors in theatrical convention, particularly in the symbolic set. He views a Royal Shakespeare Company production in 1973 as a reaction to Williams's production, but the RSC presentation did not succeed. In 1977 at the Restoration Theatre, Kennedy says, Trevor Nunn presented an *As You Like It* that was very conservative. As a reaction, Kennedy claims, Peter Stein directed a radical and memorable production at Schaubühne in West Berlin later in the same year. This production was notable, Kennedy says, for its innovative sets, its radical handling of the script, and the "bitter Arcadia" it represented.

135. Lennox, Patricia. "A Girl's Got to Eat." In *Transforming Shakespeare*, ed. Marianne Novy, 51–165. New York: St. Martin's Press, 1999.

This essay, which purports to be about eating as a metaphor in Christine Edzard's film of *As You Like It* in 1992, is really an enthusiastic and detailed review of the film. Lennox explains that Edzard locates the Forest of Arden in the Rotherhithe dock lands outside London, "an outpost of free urban space in England's post-Thatcher world of big-money high rises" (51), where both Rosalind and Orlando experience an exhilarating freedom. Lennox praises the feminist interpretation of *As You Like It* in Edzard's casting "strong actresses who give their parts specific characteristics and establish identifiable personalities that are well maintained" (59). This is as true for Phebe and Audrey as for Celia and Rosalind, Lennox maintains. And, Lennox says, Celia's sense of desertion is skillfully conveyed. But the end of the film cuts the appearance of Hymen, Jacques's blessings, and Rosalind's epilogue, and the result, Lennox claims, is a conclusion which puts in place all the patriarchal hierarchy. For further comments on this film, see Marriette (no. 136) and Coursen (no. 195).

136. Marriette, Amelia. "Urban Dystopias: Reapproaching Christine Edzard's *As You Like It*." In *Shakespeare, Film,* Fin de Siècle, ed. Mark T. Burnett and Ramona Wray, 73–88. London: Macmillan, 2000.

For Marriette, Edzard's 1992 film "emerges as experimental and challenging, a work by a relatively emancipated film maker which dispenses with convention and tradition to create a unique Shakespearean utterance" (73). The most radical feature of the film is, according to Marriette, the location of Arden in the dock lands outside London and the contrast between the corporate world and the urban wasteland. In using this setting, Marriette asserts, Edzard shows the futility of the utopian impulse and links her film to other dystopian films, such as Oliver Stone's *Wall Street* of 1987. This division of the city is complemented, according to Marriette, "by the doubling of nearly all of the main characters" (83), and the effect is intensified by costuming Rosalind and Orlando so that they "become mirror images of one another" (84). "Even in the final moments," Marriette concludes, "the film settles into no tidy interpretive arrangement" (86). For further comments on this film, see Lennox (no. 135) and Coursen (no. 195).

137. Rickman, Alan. "Jacques." In *Players of Shakespeare 2: Further Essays* *in Shakespearean Performance by Players with the Royal Shakespeare Company*, ed. Robert Smallwood, 73-80. Cambridge: Cambridge Univ. Press, 1988.

Rickman played Jacques in Adrian Noble's production of 1985. He found it a lonely part to play, but observes that "a curious complicity is established with the audience which allows a lot of warmth in" (79). He also notes that playing Jacques made him realize how little Duke Senior learns from his experience in Arden.

138. Rutter, Carol. "Rosalind: Iconoclast in Arden." In *Clamorous Voices: Shakespeare's Women Today*, ed. Faith Evans, 97-121. New York: Routledge, 1989.

Rutter interviews Juliet Stevenson about playing Rosalind and about the 1985 production of *As You Like It* in general. Stevenson asserts the iconoclasm she finds in the play against both Shakespeare and the director Adrian Noble, who, she believes, are more conservative than she is. Not only is Rosalind iconoclastic, as she debunks romantic myths to achieve a clear-eyed sense of what love means; but, according to Stevenson, the play questions stereotypes as well: "It isn't about confirming cosy opinions or settled stereotypes. It isn't about a woman in search of romantic love. The search is for knowledge and for faith—and in that search Rosalind is clamorous." (121) For a negative view of this performance and of the character, see Hamer, no. 132.

139. Shaw, Fiona, and Juliet Stevenson. "Celia and Rosalind." In *Players of Shakespeare 2: Further Essays in Shakespearean Performance by Players with the Royal Shakespeare Company*, ed. Robert Smallwood, 55-72. Cambridge: Cambridge Univ. Press, 1988.

Shaw and Stevenson played Celia and Rosalind in Adrian Noble's production of 1985. They remark on the fact that the relationship between Celia and Rosalind is unparalleled in Shakespeare and that the acting problems are mostly Celia's, due to her long periods of listening to dialogue between Rosalind and Orlando. They provide an insight into the possibility that Celia's isolation in Arden as Rosalind's romance develops makes Celia instantly ready for loving Oliver.

140. Stamm, Rudolph. *Shakespeare's Word Scenery with Some Remarks on Stage History and the Interpretation of His Plays.* Zürich and St. Gallen: Polygraphischer Verlag, 1954.

Stamm uses *As You Like It*, among other plays, to show how Shakespeare establishes location and sets scenes in his text. Stamm argues that modern realistic stage machinery creates a redundancy to the text and that modern productions often render the lines inaudible. His arguments provide an important perspective on modern productions.

141. Tennant, David. "Touchstone in *As You Like It*." In *Players of Shakespeare 4: Further Essays in Shakespearian Performance by Players with the Royal Shakespeare Company*, ed. Robert Smallwood, 30–44. Cambridge: Cambridge Univ. Press, 1998.

Tennant played Touchstone in Steven Pimlott's production of 1996, and he emphasizes the baggage that goes along with playing a famous Shakespearean role: "Be funny or sink" (31). He explores all the reasons why Touchstone's part had not seemed funny to him, but he concludes that "I've gradually discovered that Shakespeare's clowns *are* funny!" (44).

142. Thompson, Sophie. "Rosalind (and Celia)." In *Players of Shakespeare 3: Further Essays in Shakespearian Performance by Players with the Royal Shakespeare Company*, ed. Robert Smallwood, 77–86. Cambridge: Cambridge Univ. Press, 1990.

Thompson played Rosalind in John Caird's RSC production of *As You Like It* in 1989, after having played Celia in an earlier production by the Renaissance Theatre Company. Watching Rosalind from Celia's vantage made her aware, Thompson says, of Rosalind's dark side, and more sensitive than she would have been to Rosalind's interest in Jacques.

143. Ward, John Powell. *The Stage History and the Critical Reception of "As You Like It."* Harvester New Critical Introductions to Shakespeare. New York & London: Harvester Wheatsheaf, 1992.

Ward provides a sketch of stage history and critical reception. There is little performance until 1740 and little commentary as well. Productions are plentiful after the mid-eighteenth century, but serious criticism awaits the twentieth century. Ward's readings are theoretically informed, eclectic, and sensitive to issues of gender. After having analyzed most of the characters, Arden, and many of the symbols, Ward concludes, "Everything is said indirectly" (90). "'The poet affirmes nothing, and therefore never lyeth,' as Sir Philip Sidney has it" (92).

144. Wickham, Glynne. "Reflections Arising from Recent Productions of *Love's Labour's Lost* and *As You Like It*." In *Shakespeare and the Sense of Performance*, ed. Marvin and Ruth Thompson, 210–18. Newark: Delaware Univ. Press, 1989. Repr. in Tomarken (no. 152).

Wickham addresses the problem of identifying *Love's Labour's Won*, listed as one of Shakespeare's plays in *Palladis Tamia* (1598) by Francis Meres. None of the middle comedies is listed by Meres, and both *As You*

Like It and *Much Ado* have been candidates for *Love's Labour's Won*. Wickham begins his argument for *As You Like It* with the suggestion that *Love's Labour's Lost*, which is listed by Meres, invites a return of the principals in a year and a day. And having directed both *Love's Labour's Lost* and *As You Like It* in the same year, Wickham is struck by the similarities of the four couples in each play, the woodland settings, the echo of the sonnet scene in *Love's Labour's Lost* in the sonnets Orlando hangs on trees, and the similarities of Don Armado to Jacques. Wickham speculates that the boy who played the French Princess suffered a voice change, and so Rosaline, Katherine, and Maria became Rosalind, Celia, and Phebe, while Jacquenetta became Audrey. This argument has implications for the date of composition of *As You Like It* because the play is absent from Meres's list and usually dated 1599–1600. For arguments that *As You Like It* may be *Love's Labours Won*, see Knowles (no. 89); for arguments that *Much Ado* may be *Love's Labour's Won*, see Furness (no. 156).

See also nos. 66–76.

G. Adaptations.

145. Holding, Edith. "*As You Like It* Adapted: Johnson's *Love in a Forest*." *Shakespeare Survey* 32 (1979): 37–48.

Charles Johnson's adaptation was given six performances in 1723. Holding argues that adaptations were viewed as necessary to adjust Shakespeare to contemporary taste for unity and simplicity—and to politicize the text. She notes that the adaptation omits several characters and imports lines from five other Shakespeare plays. "Shakespeare serves Johnson's purpose well, providing him with no less than six sources for a concoction vastly different from any of them. The resulting adaptation is ingenious, even innovatory. Curious and eclectic as *Love in a Forest* may seem, it represents the undoubted preference of eighteenth-century audiences for whom *As You Like It* itself was as yet unacceptably complex." (48) For the text of the play, see Johnson (no. 146); for further commentary, see Maurer (no. 147) and Scheil (no. 148).

146. Johnson, Charles. *Love in a Forest.* London: W. Chetwood, 1723. Facsimile reprint: London: Cornmarket, 1969. Repr. in Tomarken (no. 152).

This adaptation follows the eighteenth-century practice of altering and combining Shakespeare's texts to produce a work adjusted to the taste of its audience. Johnson cuts Touchstone, Audrey, Silvius, Phebe, Sir Oliver Martext, and makes Jacques the mate to Celia. He ends the play with "Pyramus and Thisbe" from *A Midsummer's Night's Dream*. For commentary on the play, see Holding (no. 145), Maurer (no. 147), and Scheil (no. 148).

147. Maurer, Margaret. "Facing the Music in Arden: 'Twas I, But 'Tis not I.'" In *"As You Like It" from 1660 to the Present*, ed. Edward Tomarken, 475–509. New York: Garland, 1997 (no. 152).

Maurer compares *As You Like It* to Charles Johnson's *Love in a Forest* and the preferences of Pope, whose edition of Shakespeare appeared in the same year as Johnson's play, 1723. She finds that Johnson's changes often solve staging problems which Shakespeare's text poses for a small acting company, while also conforming to Pope's taste. She concludes "that the play's essential conceit, embodied in the elements of the stylized theatre for which it was created, is unusually open to anything those who play with it can imagine, finally all but indifferent to what is or what should be" (508). For the text of the play, see Johnson (no. 146); for further commentary, see Holding (no. 145) and Scheil (no. 148).

148. Scheil, Katherine West. "Early Georgian Politics and Shakespeare: The Black Act and Charles Johnson's *Love in a Forest*." *Shakespeare Survey* 51 (1998): 45–56.

Scheil claims that Charles Johnson's adaptation of *As You Like It* (with additions from other Shakespeare plays) was a response to a political crisis involving Jacobitism and the Blacks, poachers in black face who roamed the forests around 1720. The Black Act was passed in 1723, shortly after the premiere of *Love in a Forest*. According to Scheil, the play creates, through expansion and change in Jacques's role, "a spokesman who generates sympathy for the Whig government's actions against the Blacks" (53). Scheil also argues that "by presenting *Love in a Forest* as a rescued play of Shakespeare's, Johnson taps into the cultural resonance of the developing 'National Poet'" (56). For the text of the play, see Johnson (no. 146).

H. Collections.

149. Bloom, Harold, ed. *Rosalind*. New York: Chelsea House, 1992.

The collection is one of a series edited by Bloom that presents commentary on outstanding literary characters. For Bloom, Rosalind and Falstaff are the two comedic Shakespeare characters that rival Hamlet in scope and inventiveness, if not in philosophic depth. The collection contains selections from the work of C. L. Barber (no. 28), Edward Berry (no. 92), William C. Carroll (no. 118), Walter Davis, Charles Forker, Marjorie Garber (no. 119), H. C. Goddard (no. 49), R. Chris Hassel, Devon Hodges, and Camille Paglia. For dissent on the attractions of Rosalind, see Hamer (no. 132).

150. Halio, Jay L., ed. *Twentieth Century Interpretations of "As You Like It."* Englewood Cliffs, N.J.: Prentice-Hall, 1968.

Halio's introduction emphasizes the balance among couples in attitudes toward love—from Petrarchan posturing to simple lust—with the complex blend of impulses represented in Rosalind and Orlando. The collection contains excerpts from twentieth-century essays by C. L. Barber (no. 28) S. L. Bethell, J. R. Brown (no. 46), H. B. Charlton, Helen Gardner (no. 120), Jay Halio (no. 122), Harold Jenkins (no. 123), and Marco Mincoff (no. 102).

151. Scott, Mark W., *"As You Like It."* In *Shakespearean Criticism: Excerpts from the Criticism of William Shakespeare's Plays and Poetry from the First Published Appraisals to Current Evaluations,* 5:11–178. Detroit: Gale Research Company, 1987.

This is an extensive collection of excerpts and summaries of scholarship and criticism from 1710 to 1985. Substantial selections come from the work of Charles Gildon (1710), Richard Hurd (1753), Francis Gentleman (1770), Elisabeth Griffith (1775), William Richardson (1780), Walter Whiter (1794), S. T. Coleridge (1808), A. W. Schlegel (1811), William Hazlitt (1817), George Daniel (1829), Anna Jameson (1833), William Maginn (1837), Herman Ulrici (1839), G. G. Gervinus (1849), M. C. Clarke (1863), H. N. Hudson (1872), Edward Dowden (1881), Helena Faucit (1884), Henry Clapp (1885), H. H. Furness (1890), D. J. Snider (1890), Georg Brandes (1895), Bernard Shaw (1896), Frederick Boas (1896), E. K. Chambers (1905), S. A. Brooke (1905), E. E. Stoll (1906 and 1937), W. W. Greg (1906), Sir Arthur Quiller-Couch (1917), G. F. Bradby (1929), J. W. Draper (1934), Z. S. Fink (1935), O. J. Campbell (1935), P. V. Kreider (1935), Enid Welsford (no. 37), Mark Van Doren (no. 63), C. L. Barber (no. 28), Warren Staebler (1949), S. C. Sen Gupta (1950), H. C. Goddard (no. 49), Milton Crane (1951), Harold Jenkins (no. 123), Helen Gardner (no. 120), Geoffrey Bush (1955), J. R. Brown (no. 46), Bertrand Evans (no. 48), Jay Halio (no. 122), J. Dover Wilson (1962), G. K. Hunter (1962), Jan Kott (no. 54), Peter Philias (1966), Sylvan Barnet (no. 115), D. J. Palmer (no. 104), A. R. Cirillo (no. 93), H. M. Richmond (1971), David Young (no. 110), Patrick Swinden (no. 126), Alexander Leggatt (no. 56),

Nancy Hayles (no. 51), Elliot Krieger (no. 55), Kenneth Muir (1979), A. P. Riemer (1980), L. A. Montrose (no. 103), Alice-Lyle Scoufos (no. 105), Robert Kimbrough (no. 53), Robert Wilcher (no. 65), and Peter Erickson (no. 95). Scott presents a prefatory essay that covers the date of composition, the text, sources, and critical history.

152. Tomarken, Edward, ed. *"As You Like It" from 1660 to the Present: Critical Essays.* New York: Garland, 1997.

This collection contains much material not reprinted before. Complete documents included are as follows: Charles Johnson's *Love in a Forest* (1723), Samuel Johnson's edition of the play (1765), the introduction to *As You Like It* from J. Payne Collier's *The Works of William Shakespeare* (1842), the chapter on *As You Like It* from H. P. Ulrici's *Shakespeare's Dramatic Art* (1876), Grace Latham's lecture to the New Shakespeare Society in 1890 on Rosalind, Celia, and Helen (*All's Well*), Rosa E. Grindon's "Shakespeare and his Plays from a Woman's Point of View" (1930), Margaret Maurer's "Facing the Music in Arden" (no. 147), Jeanne A. Roberts's "Shakespearean Comedy and Some Eighteenth-Century Actresses" (1983), J. C. Bulman's "*As You Like It* and the Perils of the Pastoral" (no. 128), Glynne Wickham's "Reflections Arising from Recent Productions of *Love's Labour's Lost* and *As You Like It*" (no. 144), and Michael Jamieson's "*As You Like It*—Performance and Reception" (no. 133). Substantial excerpts are included from the work of Charles Gildon (1710), Francis Gentleman (1770), Edward Capell (1779), Walter Whiter (1794), G. G. Gervinus (1863), Denton J. Snider (1877), W. E. Henley (1888), Helena Faucit (1891), Charles Wingate (1895), Georg Brandes (1898), Austin Brereton (1908), J. B. Priestly (1925), Philip Brockbank (1985), Anthony Dawson (no. 67), and Susan Willis (1991). Brief selections are included from the work of John Masefield (1911), Charles Herford (1912), Brander Matthews (1913), Victor Freeburg (1915), Richmond Noble (1923), F. C. Kolbe (1930), Cumberland Clark (1936), George Gordon (1944), Ralph Berry (1989), Alan Dessen (1990), and from "Music and Shakespeare" (1990). Reviews of productions are included from *The Times* in 1786, 1788, 1789, 1842, 1919, *The Gentleman's Magazine* in 1741, *The London Gazette* in 1786, *The Athenaeum* in 1890, *The Spectator* in 1961, and in addition, "Shaw on Shakespear" from 1890–97 and Ellen Terry on Helena Faucit as Rosalind in 1908.

Tomarken's introduction is a detailed account of the fortunes of *As You Like It* on stage and among critics for four centuries. He says, "The result of my method is a sort of historical dialogue between the critics and theater people, reviewers, actors, actresses, producers, and directors, that demonstrates how all interpretive insights have vantage points and blind spots. *As You Like It* becomes a prism of theatrical and literary criticism of the past four centuries." (3) Tomarken is highly skilled at representing a variety of opinions in any given era. This collection is an excellent resource for the user who has a good grasp of English literary history.

I. Bibliography and Concordance.

153. Halio, Jay L., and Barbara C. Millard. *"As You Like It": An Annotated Bibliography, 1940-1980.* New York: Garland Publishing, 1985.

This volume offers a comprehensive introduction that contains discussions of genre, of the influence of romance, of the pastoral element, of fortune and nature, of courtship and the Petrarchan tradition, of the dark side of the play, of role-playing, of Shakespeare's use of sources, of rhetorical elements, of music and song, of the characters of Rosalind, Jacques, and Touchstone, of the date, of the Folio text, of the history of modern editions, and a brief history of stage and film performances. In compiling the 1584 items with annotations, the editors have been selective for the period from 1623 to 1940, and then as inclusive as possible for the years 1940-80. They have also included items reprinted in the later period. The divisions of the entries are criticism, sources and background, dating, textual criticism, texts and editions, stage history, performance criticism, films and television, influences, song collections, adaptations, bibliographies. There is also an index of actors compiled according to role. The section on performance is rich in contemporary reviews.

154. Howard-Hill, T. H., ed. *"As You Like It": A Concordance to the Text of the First Folio.* Oxford: Clarendon, 1969.

A separate volume is devoted to each of the twenty-four plays in the Oxford Shakespeare Concordances, which are based on the Oxford Old Spelling Shakespeare. "The concordance to AYL was prepared from the Lee facsimile of the First Folio (Oxford, 1902)" (xi). The volume "takes account of every word in the text, and represents their occurrence by frequency counts, line numbers, and reference lines, or a selection of these according to the interest of the particular word" (v).

See also nos. 82-86.

IV. MUCH ADO ABOUT NOTHING

A. Editions.

155. Cox, John F., ed. *Much Ado about Nothing.* Shakespeare in Production Series. Cambridge: Cambridge Univ. Press, 1997.

In addition to a lengthy introduction listing and describing productions of *Much Ado* from 1598 to 1996, the edition provides notes to the text on how various actors have interpreted lines, how scenes have been blocked, how settings were used, how actors used gestures, and more. Cox includes a bibliography of acting editions, promptbooks, and other works, largely, but not exclusively, theatrical. The text is the New Cambridge Shakespeare (1988), edited by F. H. Mares (no. 157). This edition is invaluable for those interested in Shakespeare in performance, but it is also aimed at all theatergoers.

156. Furness, Horace Howard, ed. *Much Ado About Nothing.* A New Variorum Edition of Shakespeare. New York: Lippincott, 1899. Repr. New York: Dover Publications, 1964.

In the notes to the text Furness presents not only textual variants in the Quarto and major editions of the play (listed in "The Plan of Work"), but also readings from available scholarship and other texts and documents of the period. The text is the First Folio, which Furness judges to be based on the Quarto (1600). The appendix includes comments on the text; discussion of date of composition (1599–1600); and excerpts from the sources of the plot: Harington's translation of *Orlando Furioso* (Book 5), *The Fairie Queene* 2.4, and Bandello's twentieth novella, translated by John Payne in 1890. Furness also includes Belle-Forest's version of Bandello, two analogues, and two possible sources for Bandello. English criticism of the eighteenth and nineteenth centuries is included, as are German and French criticism, stage criticism of performances by Garrick, Pritchard, Woffington, Faucit, Jordan, Macready, Irving, and Terry, and a short description of James Miller's adaptation, *The Universal Passion* (no. 205).

157. Mares, F. H., ed. *Much Ado about Nothing*. The New Cambridge Shakespeare. Cambridge: Cambridge Univ. Press, 1988.

The New Cambridge Shakespeare updates the New Shakespeare (no. 158). This edition "aims to be of value to a new generation of playgoers and readers who wish to enjoy fuller access to Shakespeare's poetic and dramatic art.... [I]t reflects current critical interests and is more attentive ... to the realisation of the plays on the stage, and to their social and cultural settings." (v) The introduction deals with sources, including Bandello, Ariosto, analogues in *The Fairie Queene*, Whetstone's *The Rock of Regard*, as well as *The Courtier* for Beatrice and Benedick; the date of the play (1600); stage history from 1613 to 1982, with illustrations. Mares offers a history of criticism, which acknowledges post-structuralism, feminist criticism, semiotics, but hews to a conventional reading of the play. A note on the text explains that the quarto of 1600 is the basis for the First Folio and provides information about compositors and a rationale for decisions made about the text presented in the edition. This edition provides rich glosses, even of characters' names. The notes set scenes, read metaphors, and explain gestures. Allusions are well documented. Appendix 1 provides the time scheme of the action. Appendix 2 presents Lewis Carroll's letter to Ellen Terry on problems in the plot. Appendix 3 provides the setting for Benedick's song (5.2.18–22).

158. Quiller-Couch, Arthur, and John Dover Wilson, eds. *Much Ado about Nothing*. The New Shakespeare. Cambridge: Cambridge Univ. Press, 1953.

The text is based on the good quarto of 1600 that is also the basis for the First Folio. The introduction, written by Quiller-Couch, covers the text, dating (1598–1600), sources, the problems of credibility in the Claudio-Hero action, the closeness of the action to tragedy, problems with the wit of Beatrice and Benedick, and the play's affinities with other comedies of Shakespeare. A long appendix describes the quarto and folio texts in detail, including a hypothesis about a manuscript promptbook, prepared "with a view to stage-performance, not for publication" (93). The editors believe that the quarto of 1600 was based on a manuscript of "an old play which had been worked over and recast" (102). They speculate that the old play contained the main plot in verse and the revision of the Benedick and Beatrice scenes in prose. They believe that in the revision Shakespeare did not clear up the details of Margaret's part in the masquerade at Hero's window. Harold Child contributes an account of the play's stage history and a glossary. This edition is useful for readers with interest in textual studies. For comments about Margaret's part, see Gilbert (no. 182).

159. Zitner, Sheldon P., ed. *Much Ado about Nothing.* The Oxford Shakespeare. Oxford: Clarendon Press, 1993.

Zitner's comprehensive introduction covers many issues not usually included. There is the obligatory discussion of date (1598) and sources, in which Zitner gives detailed comparisons to Bandello, as well as Ariosto, Spenser, Whetstone, and Castiglione. In addition, the place and setting, lovers, brothers, gentlewomen, conspirators, plot construction, acts, scenes, pace, contrasts and links between scenes, and local effects are all dealt with at some length. There is an illustrated stage history, which includes a discussion of cuts made in various eras and problems of staging certain scenes. "Some Recent Directions" deals with trends in criticism and a separate Textual Introduction covers the selection of the text for the edition, as well as issues of compositors, speech prefixes, entrances and exits, and the text in the Folio. The notes provide glosses, readings of metaphors and other figures, and explanations of gestures and allusions. An appendix covers music, song, and dance.

B. Date and Text.

For discussions of the date of *Much Ado*, including the play's candidacy to be *Love's Labour's Won*, listed by Francis Meres as one of Shakespeare's plays in *Palladis Tamia* (1598), see Furness (no. 156) and Zitner (no. 159). For discussions of the text, especially theories of manuscript revision to produce the Quarto (1600), see Mares (no. 157), Quiller-Couch and Dover Wilson (no. 158), and Zitner (no. 159).

C. Influences; Sources; Historical and Intellectual Backgrounds; Topicality.

160. Dusinberre, Juliet. "Much Ado about Lying: Shakespeare and Sir John Harington in Dialogue with *Orlando Furioso.*" In *The Italian World of English Renaissance Drama*, ed. Michele Marrapodi and A. J. Hoenselaars, 239–57. Newark: Univ. of Delaware Press, 1998.

This article continues Dusinberre's exploration of the relations of Shakespeare's comedies to Harington's work (no. 94). In *Much Ado*

Dusinberre finds, in Benedick's language and rhymes, echoes of Harington's epigrams, circulated in the 1590s, and also of his translation of *Orlando Furioso*. Dusinberre also sees a "subtle interplay between the theatrical text and the text of Harington's own writings" (245). She finds a similarity between the performative element of Benedick's character and the many roles that Harington played.

161. Gough, Melinda J. "'Her filthy feature open showne' in Ariosto, Spenser, and *Much Ado about Nothing*." *Studies in English Literature 1500-1900* 39 (1999): 41-67.

Gough traces the theme of "the beautiful enchantress exposed as a whorish hag" in *Orlando Furioso* and *The Fairie Queene* to argue that "the juxtaposition in *Much Ado* between Don John's false exposure of a whorish Hero and Claudio's subsequent attempt to shame Hero by revealing her alleged falsehood to a wide audience further elucidates not only Shakespeare's critique of epic-romance violence but his implicit response to contemporary attacks on the stage" (44). Gough also relates the difficulty Claudio and Don Pedro have in understanding Hero's character to the ambiguity of the enchantress-hag tradition. For comments on violence in romances, see Traugott (no. 170).

162. Howard, Jean E. "Renaissance Antitheatricality and the Politics of Gender and Rank in *Much Ado about Nothing*." In *Shakespeare Reproduced: The Text in History and Ideology*, ed. Jean E. Howard and Marion F. O'Connor, 163-87. London: Routledge, 1990. Repr. in Wynne-Davies (no. 211).

Howard seeks to relate *Much Ado* to the antitheatrical discourse of Shakespeare's time, with its fear of destabilizing the social order through violation of sumptuary laws and cross dressing, and to the similar arguments of tracts that castigate women who use cosmetics. Howard notes that theatrical deceptions are central to both the main plot and the trick on Beatrice and Benedick. Don Pedro promotes both marriages, but Don John uses a masquerade to "thwart his brother's fictions" (173). Howard challenges the critical position that distinguishes between the theatrical practices on the basis of morality. Don John's ruse works, she says, because "it easily passes in Messina as a truthful reading of women" (175). Moreover, Don John is himself a testimony to women's frailty. By placing Beatrice and Benedick in love discourses, Don Pedro's tricks discipline them, according to Howard, and lead them to submit to authority and the institution of marriage. At the end of the play Hero is still "the blank sheet upon which men write whore or goddess as their fears or desires dictate" (181). For further comments on antitheatrical discourse, see Myhill (no. 165).

163. Lewalski, Barbara K. "Love, Appearance and Reality: Much Ado about Something." *Studies in English Literature 1500–1900* 8 (1968), 235–51.

Lewalski reads *Much Ado* in light of Cardinal Bembo's Neoplatonic discourse on love in Book IV of *The Courtier*, which defines love in relationship to kinds of knowledge. According to Lewalski, Beatrice and Benedick act out the pattern of Bembo's rational lovers, attaining therefore an intuitive understanding of the truth. Claudio is at first moved by desire and passion, Lewalski says, but he progresses to a higher understanding and acceptance of the veiled lady on faith. Hero's feigned death is a figure for love as a redemptive sacrifice. The true instinct granted the foolish Watch comes, says Lewalski, not from Bembo, but from St. Paul (I Cor. i. 18–19). For Neoplatonism in *As You Like It*, see Scoufos (no. 105).

164. McEachern, Claire. "Fathering Herself: A Source Study of Shakespeare's Feminism." *Shakespeare Quarterly* 39 (1988): 269–90.

McEachern uses comparisons found in sources for *Much Ado* and *Lear* to argue that, in his portraits of the abuse of a father's power by Lear and Leonato, Shakespeare interrogates the patriarchal cultural order. Leonato's development from his total rejection of Hero in the church to being her chivalric champion reveals the "costs of constructing and maintaining his patriarchy" (280). McEachern points out that Hero and Leonato are never reconciled; Antonio gives her as his daughter in the second wedding.

165. Myhill, Nova. "Spectatorship in/of *Much Ado about Nothing*." *Studies in English Literature 1500–1900* 39 (1999): 291–311.

Myhill frames her detailed commentary on the spectacles in *Much Ado* with observations from the anti-theatrical discourse of the period. She concludes, "*Much Ado* is centrally concerned with problems of knowledge and perception. The representation of multiple deceptions reveals a mechanism of creating methods of interpretation—the process by which narratives ensure particular readings of spectacles, at times in the face of other equally possible interpretations. The theatre audience's assumption of its own privileged position is undercut by the frequency with which the play's characters are deceived by their assumptions that eavesdropping offers unproblematic access to truth." (292) For further comment on antitheatrical discourse, see Howard (no. 162).

166. Osborne, Laurie E. "Dramatic Play in *Much Ado about Nothing*: Wedding the Italian Novella and English Comedy." *Philological Quarterly* 69 (1990): 167-88.

Osborne speculates that both plots—Hero and Claudio, Beatrice and Benedick—derive from the slandered maiden story of Ariosto and Bandello, but the Beatrice and Benedick action works by comic principles and is the inverse of the Hero-Claudio action. The ending, says Osborne, requires a convergence of elements: Dogberry to find Don John's practice, the Friar's trick of Hero's "death," and Leonato's sentence of Claudio to expiation. For comments on the romance background of the slander, see Gough (no. 161).

167. Prouty, Charles T. *The Sources of "Much Ado about Nothing": A Critical Study, Together with the Text of Peter Beverley's "Ariodanto and Ieneura."* New Haven: Yale Univ. Press, 1950.

Prouty's comparison of *Much Ado* with its sources and analogues turns quickly into an argument about the characters of Claudio, Beatrice, and Benedick. For Prouty, Claudio is defensible because he is not a romantic lover, but a party to an arranged marriage, which Hero would enter fraudulently if she were unchaste. Beatrice and Benedick have no identifiable source, according to Prouty, but they follow a familiar pattern—the rebel who is brought to conformity. Neither couple, Prouty says, is romantic, but both are realistic in differing ways: one about arranged marriage; the other about the emotions of love.

168. Richmond, Hugh M. "Much Ado about Notables." *Shakespeare Studies* 12 (1979), 49-64.

Richmond's approach is historical, and he finds topical characters in *Much Ado*. He connects Don John the Bastard to "Don John of Austria, the illegitimate son of Charles V, half brother of the King of Aragon (and the rest of Spain), who led the fleets of Christendom from Messina to the defeat of the Turks at Lepanto.... And he returned to Messina after his victory on 7 October 1571, under conditions analogous to those at the play's start." (50-51) Richmond claims that the historical Don John's temperament was very like that of the character. Richmond also connects Beatrice and Benedick to figures from the court of Francis I, described by his sister Marguerite de Navarre in her *Heptameron*, and made accessible to Shakespeare in Painter's *Palace of Pleasure*.

169. Salingar, Leo. "Borachio's Indiscretion." In *The Italian World of English Renaissance Drama*, ed. Michele Marrapodi and A. J. Hoenselaars,

225–38. Newark: Univ. of Delaware Press, 1998.

Salingar argues that several early incidents in *Much Ado* "form a prelude and a social setting for the main intrigues that are to follow, based upon planted eavesdropping and provoked misconception: much ado about *noting*. The scene of Borachio's indiscretion is both a turning point and a climactic instance in this process of socialized distortion; a would-be confidence conveyed in the garbled words of a drunkard is made public through the blunder of eavesdroppers" (228). Salingar argues that Shakespeare changes the characterization and the tone of Bandello, particularly with regard to Leonato and Claudio. The play, he says, stresses courtly wit: "The sophisticated speakers of *Much Ado* are engaged with wit as a mark of *savoir faire* and a social game, where players repeatedly and competitively outgo plain statement" (235–6).

170. Traugott, John. "Creating a Rational Rinaldo: A Study in the Mixture of the Genres of Comedy and Romance in *Much Ado about Nothing*." *Genre* 15 (1982): 157–81.

Traugott sees the "Kill Claudio" episode as one in which Beatrice uses the romance command of service to a lady as a game "to redress a world that has no sense in it" (174). In this way, Beatrice takes over the plot and creates Benedick as a rational Rinaldo, a romance hero who defends chaste ladies. Claudio also comes from romance, including its absolutes and its violence, but he "has the luck," according to Traugott, "to find himself in a comedy" (175). Shakespearean romantic comedy is new in that it takes its high comedy figures from romance, Traugott says, but Shakespeare is also more modern than Spenser or Sidney in that he sees the cruelty and violence in romance. For further comments on "Kill Claudio," see Cox (no. 192) and Steed (no. 202).

D. Language and Linguistics.

171. Barish, Jonas. "Pattern and Purpose in the Prose of *Much Ado About Nothing*. *Rice Univ. Studies* 60 (1974): 19–30.

Barish argues that characters' speech patterns provide the audience with indications of their natures. Leonato and Don Pedro have "a complacent tendency to rest in mere words" (21), especially in complimentary phrases, while Don John's language shows that he sees the world in "sharp and irreconcilable contrarities" (21). Like other characters, Beatrice and Benedick use syntactic symmetry, but "they practice it with a playfulness that allows it to develop freely as an instrument of criticism and wit"

(24). Beatrice's speech is more open than Benedick's, according to Barish, and this difference betrays Benedick's greater self-absorption. As they drop their defenses, both Beatrice and Benedick speak more simply until Beatrice's famous outburst in the church. Here she makes wit the instrument of her anger. "In doing so," Barish argues, "she confers a positive value on wit that Benedick has retreated from, using it not for exhibitionism but for loyalty, not for swashbuckling but to express anger that a man can express, if he chooses, with his sword" (29).

172. Cerasano, S. P. "Half a Dozen Dangerous Words." In *Gloriana's Face: Women, Public and Private, in the English Renaissance*, ed. S. P. Cerasano and Marion Wynne-Davies, 167–83. London: Hemel Hempstead, 1992. Repr. in Wynne-Davies (no. 211).

Cerasano argues that *Much Ado* dramatizes the plight of women coping with slander within the actual legal structure of early modern England: women who were slandered could not defend themselves without a male advocate, and a single woman could not be compensated if she was slandered as a "whore." Claudio's slander of Hero in the church, Cerasano holds, unifies the male community against her, including her own father; Hero's swoon is a metaphorical death of the outcast. Messina's social code, according to Cerasano, becomes less attractive to the audience as the denizens accept slander and fictional death on slight evidence. And Beatrice, as a woman, is powerless to act on Hero's behalf. Cerasano argues that, in unmasking, Hero frees the men and women from the rhetoric that has bound them.

173. Jorgensen, Paul A. "Much Ado About *Nothing*." *Shakespeare Quarterly* 5 (1954): 287–95.

About *nothing*, Jorgensen writes of "the larger web of meaning which lay behind Shakespeare's remarkable insistence on the word" (287). Jorgensen reviews the prominent use of the word in *King Lear* and various other Shakspeare plays, as well as in contemporary poems. He ends with references to *Much Ado*, observing that Richard Grant White proposed in 1857 that "the original audience both pronounced and interpreted the title as 'much ado about noting'; for noting, or observing and eavesdropping, is found in almost every scene and is indispensable to all the plots" (294). Jorgensen hopes that weight may be given White's idea by "awareness of the various Nothing discourses" (295). Clearly this was an idea awaiting its time. For further comments on *noting*, see Salingar (no. 169), Dawson (no. 179), Hockey (no. 183), Jenkins (no. 185), and Rossiter (no. 189).

174. McCollum, W. G. "The Role of Wit in *Much Ado About Nothing.*" *Shakespeare Quarterly* 19 (1968): 165–74. Repr. in Davis (no. 210).

McCollum announces his thesis: "The wit of Shakespeare's play informs the words spoken by the characters, places the characters themselves as truly witty and intelligent, inappropriately facetious, or ingeniously witless, suggests the lines of action these characters will take, and, as intelligence, plays a fundamental role in the thematic action: the triumphing of true wit (or wise folly) in alliance with harmless folly over false or pretentious wisdom" (166). McCollum classifies the technique of wit in four types: verbal identifications and contrasts; conceptual wit; flights of fancy; and parodies and burlesques. He gives several examples of each. For McCollum, the merry war of true wit between Beatrice and Benedick is contrasted to the hollow rhetoric of Claudio, Don Pedro, and Leonato, and the use of wit by Don Pedro and Claudio after Hero's "death" illustrates their callousness.

175. Spurgeon, Caroline. "*Much Ado.*" In *Shakespeare's Imagery and What It Tells Us*, 263–66. Cambridge: Cambridge Univ. Press, 1935.

Spurgeon describes the large number of lively images from dance, music, riding, and animal movement in *Much Ado*. The play is dominated, she says, by images of English country life, especially outdoor sports, which are important in *Much Ado* "for the only time in Shakespeare's plays" (264).

See also nos. 39–41, 140.

E. Criticism.

176. Allen, John A. "Dogberry." *Shakespeare Quarterly* 24 (1973): 35–53.

For Allen, Dogberry is central to *Much Ado* because he epitomizes the inflated ego of the culture of Messina. "He is the gross exemplar of an attitude which is endemic there" (37). Dogberry, says Allen, has every confidence in his superior wisdom, and in this and in the way he exercises authority he is very like Leonato. Allen claims that *Much Ado's* "view of human nature, for all the barbs of satire which it looses, is a tolerant one" (53). For further comments on Dogberry, see Smith (no. 190).

177. Berger, Harry. "Against the Sink-a-Pace: Sexual and Family Politics in *Much Ado about Nothing.*" In *Making Trifles of Terrors: Redistributing Complicities in Shakespeare*, 10–24. Stanford: Stanford Univ. Press, 1997. Repr. in Wynne-Davies (no. 211).

Berger argues that Hero is more self-aware than she is usually portrayed. "Even this most male-dominated of heroines betrays more than once her sense of her complicity in the sexual politics of Messina" (11). According to Berger, Hero becomes frisky and flirtatious at times, especially during the gulling of Beatrice. This behavior prepares the audience for the "new Hero," who "is more than a match for Claudio" at the end of the play (24).

178. Cook, Carol. "'The Sign and Semblance of Her Honor': Reading Gender Difference in *Much Ado about Nothing*." *PMLA* 101 (1986): 186–202.

In a Freudian reading of the play, Cook declares, "I argue that the play masks, as well as exposes, the mechanisms of masculine power and that insofar as it avoids what is crucial to its conflicts, the explicitly offered comic resolution is something of an artful dodge" (186). Cook asserts that the cuckold jokes restore threatened male prerogative by returning women to silence, authorizing male fantasies of women, and building male camaraderie. She says, "The woman is doubly threatening, both in her imagined capacity to betray and cuckold men and as an image of what men fear to become: paradoxically, her very vulnerability is threatening" (189). For Cook, Hero is the "nothing" which generates much ado, the silent cipher to be read by the other characters, who make her the chaste Diana or the treacherous Venus. The pretence of Hero's death, Cook says, simply redefines her as chaste, but does not change the patriarchal dualism. For Cook, Margaret and Don John, as scapegoats, carry away any guilt from Don Pedro and Claudio.

179. Dawson, Anthony B. "Much Ado About Signifying." *Studies in English Literature 1500–1900* 22 (1982): 211–21.

This is possibly the earliest of many studies of *Much Ado* as a play "in which attention is directed as much to the way meaning is produced as to what the meaning is" (211). Messages are constantly intercepted, misinterpreted, called into question, overheard, says Dawson. Frequent eavesdropping calls attention to the fact that "messages become in themselves signs as well as vehicles, of the major concerns of the play" (214). The article ends with an extended comparison of Claudio and Othello.

180. Dennis, Carl. "Wit and Wisdom in *Much Ado about Nothing*." *Studies in English Literature 1500–1900* 13 (1973): 223–37.

According to Dennis, *Much Ado* works on a distinction between wit, which depends on reason, and wisdom, which depends on faith in others. Beatrice and Benedick come to reject wit and develop faith in one another and in Hero, while Claudio's commitment to Hero is too shallow for him to overcome wit's evidence with faith. Instead, he does this symbolically: "The apparent miracle of Hero's resurrection comes about only by repudiating the kind of skeptical wit that caused her apparent death" (235). For further comments about wit, see McCollum (no. 174).

181. Everett, Barbara. "*Much Ado About Nothing*: The Unsociable Comedy." In *English Comedy*, ed. Michael Cordner, Peter Holland, and John Kerrigan, 68–84. Cambridge: Cambridge Univ. Press, 1994. Repr. in Wynne-Davies (no. 211).

Everett stresses the balance of *Much Ado* between the daily triviality of life in Messina and the serious relationship between Beatrice and Benedick, who displace Claudio and Hero as the center of the play. She sees Beatrice and Benedick as intelligent and caring people who are changed by the depths of feeling they experience in the church scene. According to Everett, Claudio's shallow love for Hero is easily destroyed, and their wedding is arranged for the stability of their society; they are still people to whom nothing can happen, while Beatrice and Benedick have the depth of feeling for romantic love and a genuine relationship.

182. Gilbert, Allan H. "Two Margarets: The Composition of *Much Ado about Nothing*." *Philological Quarterly* 41 (1962): 61–71.

When Claudio rejects Hero for talking with a man from her chamber window, Margaret does not exonerate her mistress, even though Margaret spoke to Borachio from Hero's window while dressed in Hero's clothes. So there are, Gilbert argues, two Margarets in *Much Ado*, one who has witty jousts with Beatrice and others, and another who appears only in narrative and is essential to the plot. Although the discrepancy, which seems to be the result of numerous revisions of the text, is apparent when the play is read, Gilbert believes that it has never bothered audiences attentive to the spectacular church scene. For the textual background of Gilbert's argument, see Quiller-Couch and Dover Wilson (no. 158).

183. Hockey, Dorothy C. "Notes, Notes, Forsooth...." *Shakespeare Quarterly* 8 (1957): 353–58. Repr. in Davis (no. 210).

Hockey argues that "*Much Ado* is a comedy of mis-noting ... the inability to observe, judge, and act sensibly" (354). She explains how each tricked character insists on the validity of his/her senses; the result is to unify the effect of the three disparate strands of action. She concludes, "There is ... a unity of plot device, as we have seen. Repeatedly Shakespeare calls our attention to it, and repeatedly he uses it for build-up as well as for major action. The over-all effect on our impression of the characters and their behavior is, I think, to draw them all together in a common plight." (357) For further comments about *noting*, see Salingar (no. 169), Jorgensen (no. 173), Dawson (no. 179), Jenkins (no. 185), and Rossiter (no. 189).

184. Huston, J. Dennis. *Shakespeare's Comedies of Play*. New York: Columbia Univ. Press, 1981.

Huston deals with playfulness in *The Comedy of Errors, Love's Labor's Lost, The Taming of the Shrew, Midsummer Night's Dream*, and *Much Ado*. Especially significant for Huston are the performances designed by Don Pedro to trick Beatrice and Benedick into admitting their love, the precise obverse of the performance of Borachio and Margaret, staged by Don John, to trap Claudio and Hero. According to Huston, *Much Ado* abounds in performances, but the world of the play proves to be too complex to be controlled by a single artistic figure. For another reading of the actions as symmetrical opposites, see Osborne (no. 166).

185. Jenkins, Harold. "*Much Ado about Nothing*." *Shakespeare Newsletter*. Extra Issue 1997, 5–7.

In a lecture delivered in 1982 and published for the first time in 1997, Jenkins stresses the importance of plot in *Much Ado* and the skill with which it is constructed. He notes that the plot of the rejected bride had recurring interest for Shakespeare, who used it six times. Jenkins admires the way in which the two couples are separated and united by a series of eavesdroppings: "The contrivances and accidents of overhearing supply the recurrent motif of the whole dramatic design; and it is clear that Shakespeare perceived and planned this from the outset" (7). Jenkins also praises the witty prose dialogue of the play: Beatrice and Benedick are blessed, he says, with speech that is endlessly inventive, and Dogberry with a "bumbling self-importance [that] exactly meets the practical dramatic requirement that the truth which must come out must not come out too soon" (7).

186. King, Walter N. "Much Ado About Something." *Shakespeare Quarterly* 15 (1964): 143–55. Repr. in Davis (no. 210).

King reads *Much Ado* as a comedy of manners in which the focus "is the critical inspection of a leisure-class world grown morally flabby by thoughtless acceptance of an inherited social code" (145). For King, characters are gradually brought to a proper norm of behavior in the denouement. King's Messina is a superficial society that breeds thoughtless conformists like Claudio and Hero; although they are people of more substance, Benedick and Beatrice are also stereotypes: the disdainful Petrarchan lady and the antifeminist windbag. During the tricks, King says they behave according to convention, but the shock of seeing the effect of wit on their personalities begins their change of heart. The church scene, King argues, ratifies their change. For Claudio, change is not possible, but a second marriage of convenience brings him into line with prevailing social codes, as much as Hero hopes for. "More significant," King argues, "is the fact that Beatrice and Benedick have developed sufficient insight into themselves to become living norms for their society instead of being carping critics of their society's norms" (155).

187. Krieger, Elliot. "Social Relations and the Social Order in *Much Ado about Nothing*." *Shakespeare Survey*, 32 (1979): 49–61.

Krieger presents a Marxist analysis of the deceptions in *Much Ado* for their social implications and concludes that only a society that does not question appearances could be so deceived. For Krieger, the social codes of Messina accept marriage as a "pinnacle of achievement for both the domestic and the military sections of society" (53), and the language of the aristocracy solidifies it and assures that surfaces will not be probed. "The play is an inquisition into the values of a society that refuses to question its values" (58). Beatrice's call for revenge comes, according to Krieger, "from her revulsion against the trivial attitudes and the social codes in her society" (59); these issues are not resolved, but dissolved by the discovery of Claudio's mistake. "*Much Ado* is a play about trivial and egotistical people whose concerns will remain superficial because of the quality of their personalities" (60).

188. Neely, Carol Thomas. "Broken Nuptials: *Much Ado about Nothing*." In *Broken Nuptials in Shakespeare's Plays*, 24–57. New Haven: Yale Univ. Press, 1985.

Neely's chapter focuses on *Much Ado* as central to the theme of broken nuptials in the comedies. For her the play extends earlier uses of the theme and anticipates the problem comedies and the tragedies. Neely says several processes must take place before a marriage can occur: separation from family, exorcism of misogyny, qualification of romantic idealization, and control of desire. In *Much Ado*, Neely argues, "The two plots release and control elements that will generate greater uneasiness and distrust in the problem comedies. Together they maintain an equilibrium between male control and female initiative, between male reform and female submission, which is characteristic of the romantic comedies but is disrupted in the problem comedies. In this play, wit clarifies the vulnerability of romantic idealization while romance alters the static, self-defensive gestures of wit." (40)

189. **Rossiter, A. P.** "*Much Ado about Nothing.*" In *Angel with Horns*, 67–81. London: Longmans, Green, 1961. Repr. in Muir (no. 81) and Davis (no. 210).

Rossiter attends carefully to the language of *Much Ado* and to the deftness of plotting, especially to interrelation of the three actions. "It seems to me that misapprehensions, misprisions, misunderstandings, misinterpretations and misapplications are the best names for what the comedy *as a whole* is all 'about'" (77). Rossiter contends that, although *Much Ado* is not a tragic play, it deals with themes "which are to have sufficiently serious explorations and consequences in Shakespeare's later work" (79). Rossiter's conclusion is psychological: *Much Ado* stands at the point where tragic potential is held off by a hardness of spirit and determined gaiety: "It is as if the sensitive mind and heart sought to persuade themselves by demonstration that life is a jest" (81). This is one of the best early essays on the dark side of *Much Ado*.

190. **Smith, James.** "*Much Ado about Nothing*". In *Shakespearian and Other Essays*, ed. E. M. Wilson, 24–72. Cambridge: Cambridge Univ. Press, 1974. Repr. in Davis (no. 210).

This essay was originally published in *Scrutiny* in 1946. It is therefore one of the earliest examinations of the superficiality of the society of Messina. Smith argues that Dogberry is far from being dispensable to the plot, as Coleridge had claimed, because Dogberry shares the exact qualities of Leonato, Claudio, and Don Pedro, a comic hubris, and a preoccupation with appearances and with social position. Smith argues that the accusation of Hero is a catalyst for the realization by Beatrice and Benedick that "life has something to offer, too valuable for its seizure to be delayed on pretexts of doubtful moment" (36). Yet, Smith says, the eavesdropping scenes show the childishness of the entire society, which the Prince and Claudio display when Benedick challenges Claudio and even more after the ruse has been discovered. Smith sees a return to status quo with relief at the end: "Messina can return to its former gaieties, all joining in a dance which, if the Dogberries are not invited to it, they would have at any rate appreciated, and which they would hardly have disgraced" (41). For further commentary on Dogberry, see Allen (no. 176).

F. Stage History and Performance Criticism.

191. Branagh, Kenneth. *"Much Ado about Nothing" by William Shakespeare: Screenplay, Introduction, and Notes on the Making of the Movie.* New York: W. W. Norton, 1993.

This amply illustrated volume contains the text of the screenplay, together with elaborate descriptions of the filming sites. In the introduction Branagh explains why he wanted to make the film and his directorial intentions. "The goal was utter reality of characterisation.... [I]t is the detail of humanity amongst the participants that helps make *Much Ado* one of Shakespeare's most accessible works." (ix) Branagh describes recruiting the international cast, and his approach to the action, emphasizing emotional volatility and rashness of men accustomed to facing death. For reviews of the film, see Coursen (no. 195), Hattaway (no. 197), and Lehmann (no. 198).

192. Cox, J. F. "The Stage Representation of the 'Kill Claudio' Sequence in *Much Ado about Nothing*." *Shakespeare Survey* 32 (1979): 27–36.

In an examination of this scene in a range of English productions from the eighteenth century to the mid-twentieth century, Cox emphasizes certain points. First, the most successful productions (those that provoke no unwanted laughter) establish a continuity between the emotions of the church scene and the ensuing dialogue. Second, tact is necessary to convey the tentativeness of Beatrice and Benedick with one another. The challenge of the scene is to maintain a balance between its serious and comic elements. The intensity of Beatrice's emotions is a challenge, as is too great aggression for Benedick. Cox argues that Gielgud's portrayal of Benedick showed how trusting the text can succeed. For a contrasting opinion, see Steed (no. 202); for use of the scene in teaching, see Hapgood (no. 208).

193. Croall, Jonathan. "Stratford and Peter Brook." In *Gielgud, A Theatrical Life*, 355–68. New York: Continuum, 2001.

Croall recounts how Gielgud's *Much Ado* at Stratford-upon-Avon in 1949 was praised by critics as among the best post-war productions. In 1950 Gielgud assumed the role of Benedick with Peggy Ashcroft as Beatrice. Croall says, "His Benedick established Gielgud's mastery of Shakespearean high comedy as never before" (359). Gielgud continued playing the role in 1952 and 1955 in London and 1959 in New York.

194. Coursen, H. R. "Anachronism and Papp's *Much Ado*." In *Shakespeare on*

Television, ed. J. C. Bulman and H. R. Coursen, 151-55. Hanover: Univ. Press of New England, 1988.

Coursen is highly critical of the Joseph Papp production of *Much Ado*, directed by A. J. Antoon in 1973, starring Kathleen Widdowes as Beatrice and Sam Waterston as Benedick. Coursen says, "The Papp-Antoon *Much Ado About Nothing* ... demolishes Shakespeare's play very effectively, but it leaves in its place a cultural disaster" (151). The major error of the production is setting the play in small-town America of 1910, according to Coursen and other critics he quotes. But, Coursen asks, if historical accuracy was not a value for Shakespeare, why fault Antoon for his setting? Because the setting "obliterates whatever Shakespeare may still be saying to us with *his* play" (153). Coursen concludes, "Conception, direction, acting and voice, accommodation to the medium—these are criteria one must consider in assessing any production of Shakespeare. Mr. Papp and Mr. Antoon fail vividly in each area." (155) This volume also contains four other reviews of this production.

195. Coursen, H. R. "Branagh's *Much Ado*." In *Shakespeare in Production, Whose History?* 90-117. Athens: Ohio Univ. Press, 1996.

Although Coursen's title suggests that he writes only of Branagh's film, he in fact contrasts Branagh's conventional art with others which challenge received opinion, such as Christine Edzard's *As You Like It*. For Coursen, Branagh's film merely ratifies what we already know. In contrast, Coursen cites liberties like Viola appearing in her wedding dress at the end of a Stratford, Ontario, *Twelfth Night* (1994) or Jacques played as gay in a Bates College *As You Like It* (1993) as examples of ways in which productions can challenge the text. Coursen provides detailed descriptions of many productions of *As You Like It* and *Twelfth Night*, including the Edzard film. In its radical setting and strong female performances, Edzard's film forms a sharp contrast to Branagh's, which hews to the tradition of Shakespeare as high culture and good taste. Coursen concludes, "The Branagh *Much Ado about Nothing*, like the 1994 RSC *Twelfth Night*, comes off as quite conventional. I suggest that we need no more 'conventional' versions of this or any script, however." (116) Coursen likes Edzard's film better than most of the critics he quotes. Like many other critics, Coursen rejects Branagh's interpretation of Dogberry.

196. Gielgud, John. "Benedick." In *Stage Directions*, 36-43. London: Heinemann, 1963.

Gielgud directed *Much Ado* at Stratford-upon-Avon in 1949. He imported a designer from Spain to create simple, but easily changed scenes that did not require a curtain. Gielgud insists that overhearing scenes be played with the target character closest to the audience. He stresses that the stage be as simple as possible because of the complexity of Shakespeare's language. He objects to changing the period of *Much Ado* to Victorian or Regency, which are not, in his view, hospitable to the bawdry of Shakespeare's language. This very successful production was revived in the fifties. For further comment on Gielgud, see Croall (no. 193).

197. Hattaway, Michael. " 'I've processed my guilt': Shakespeare, Branagh, and the Movies." In *Shakespeare and the Twentieth Century: The Selected Proceedings of the International Shakespeare Association World Congress, Los Angeles 1996*, ed. Jonathan Bate, Jill Levenson, and Dieter Mehl, 194–211. Newark: Univ. of Delaware Press, 1998.

Hattaway gives an incisive review of Branagh's *Much Ado* (1993), which he discusses in detail and dislikes: "I would argue that it is a failure to think through the ways in which Shakespearean conventions for inwardness and ludic behavior might be transformed into film that makes Branagh's *Much Ado* so unsatisfactory" (197). Hattaway is a shrewd commentator on film technique and on the cuts in Shakespeare's text Branagh made to fit the medium of film. For additional views of this film, see Branagh (no. 191), Coursen (no. 195), and Lehmann (no. 198).

198. Lehmann, Courtney. "Much Ado about Nothing? Shakespeare, Branagh, and the 'national-popular' in the age of multinational capital." *Textual Practice* 12 (1998): 1–22.

Lehmann tries to assess whether, in making his film of *Much Ado*, Branagh succeeds in realizing his vision of a Shakespeare that is "multinational popular," blending high and popular culture. Lehmann notes that the film seeks to erase class through its uniform costuming and to erase nationality in its multinational cast. But casting Denzel Washington as Don Pedro and the film's lack of satire in its parody reveal how "Branagh wants to have his other, and eat it, too" (15). Lehmann concludes, "Simultaneously the figure around whom Branagh constructs his 'progressive' multiculturalist fantasy of a 'Shakespeare film for the world' and whom the camera systematically excludes from the film's scenes of social harmony, Washington's definitively 'different' Don Pedro gives the lie to Branagh's ultimately 'regressive' vision of a multinational-popular" (2). Lehmann's discussion is theorized using Antonio Gramsci, Robert Weimann, Michel Foucault, and Frederick Jameson. For other views of this film, see Branagh (no. 191), Coursen (no. 195), and Hattaway (no. 197).

199. Mason, Pamela. *"Much Ado about Nothing": Text and Performance.* London: Macmillan, 1992.

This useful series presents a running commentary on the text of the play and a brief stage history of recent productions. In commentary on performances Mason argues that finding a setting in which Claudio's actions "can be made explicable, if not acceptable" is the challenge of the play (44). The performance history covers the following productions: Gielgud's in 1949 and later; Franco Zefferelli's at the National Theatre in 1965; Trevor Nunn's production at Stratford-upon-Avon in 1968; John Barton's Raj production with the RSC in 1976; the National Theatre production of 1981; Terry Hand's of 1982; the 1984 BBC film; the 1988 Renaissance Theatre Company directed by Judi Dench and the RSC production directed by Di Trevis in the same year; and the RSC production of 1990 directed by Bill Alexander.

200. *"Much Ado About Nothing"* (BBC 1984 [PBS, 30 November 1984]). In *Shakespeare on Television*, ed. J. C. Bulman and H. R. Coursen, 302-10. Hanover: Univ. Press of New England, 1988.

Bulman and Coursen excerpt three reviews—all positive—of this production, directed by Stuart Burge and produced by Shaun Sutton, with Cherie Lunghi as Beatrice and Robert Lindsay as Benedick. The reviews are by David Richards in *The Washington Post* 30 November 1984; Peter Kemp in *Times Literary Supplement* 11 January 1985; and Susan McCloskey in *Shakespeare on Film Newsletter* 9 (1985): 2.

201. Schafer, Elizabeth. *"Much Ado about Nothing."* In *Ms-Directing Shakespeare: Women Direct Shakespeare.* London: The Women's Press, 1998.

This chapter covers Gale Edwards's production in Adelaide in 1987; Di Trevis's production with the RSC in 1988 and Judi Dench's Renaissance Theatre Company production of the same year; and Helena Kaut-Howson's production at the Manchester Royal Exchange in 1997. Much comment is devoted to the failure with the critics of Trevis's overtly political interpretation.

202. Steed, Maggie. "Beatrice in *Much Ado About Nothing.*" In *Players of Shakespeare 3: Further essays in Shakespearian performance by players with the Royal Shakespeare Company,* ed. Russell Jackson and Robert Smallwood, 42-51. Cambridge: Cambridge Univ. Press, 1993.

Steed played Beatrice in Di Trevis's *Much Ado* in 1988. About the play in general, Steed says that Shakespeare makes us think we are safe after the war and then plunges "us all into catastrophe in our own front rooms" (43). Steed sees Beatrice as the family clown, earning her way as a dependent in Leonato's household, and defending against a deep hurt—possibly the betrayal of her mother. The pain of the church scene allows Beatrice and Benedick, Steed says, "to lower their defences and declare their love for each other" (49). In this play of surprise, it does not matter for Steed whether the audience laughs at "Kill Claudio." For another opinion of the "Kill Claudio" scene, see Cox (no. 192).

See also nos. 66, 68–75, 155.

G. Adaptations.

203. Collins, Howard S. *"The Law Against Lovers."* In *The Comedy of Sir William Davenant*, 140–48. The Hague: Mouton, 1967.

Of Davenant's adaptation, Collins says, "He wanted to ally two well-known Shakespeare plots, observing the classical unities, and elevating the moral tone. He wished also to entertain a highly homogeneous audience that did not care to be mentally taxed. Thus he proffered a complicated plot, several scenes of song and dance, and a few gobbets of such humor as he had supplied in earlier decades." (147) For the text of the play, see Davenant (no. 204); for additional criticism, see Cox (no. 155) and Scheil (no. 206).

204. Davenant, Sir William. *The Law Against Lovers.* In *Works of Sir William Davenant*, 2:272–329. 2 vols. London: H. Herringman, 1673. Repr. New York: Benjamin Blom, 1968.

This play combines *Much Ado* with *Measure for Measure*, despite the fact that Davenant held patents to stage both Shakespeare plays. The combination gave Davenant the opportunity also to add song and dance to the new work. For comments, see Odell (no. 72), Cox (no. 155), Collins (no. 203), and Scheil (no. 206).

205. Miller, James. *The Universal Passion: a Comedy.* London: J. Watts, 1737.

The play combines *Much Ado* with Moliere's *Princesse D'Elide*. Miller follows Shakespeare in placing the slander action at the center, with an assertive Hero figure, a well-motivated Don John, and a dignified Leonato. The Beatrice and Benedick figures are close to Shakespeare's, and the play ends with love and marriage vindicated. For description and comments, see Cox (no. 155) and Furness (no. 156).

206. Scheil, K. W. "Sir William Davenant's Use of Shakespeare in *The Law*

Against Lovers (1662)." *Philological Quarterly* 76 (1997): 369–86.

Scheil argues that Davenant's play, which combines *Much Ado about Nothing* with *Measure for Measure*, "marks an important moment in the history of Shakespearian reception" (380). In 1662, Scheil claims, Shakespeare's reputation was no draw to the box office. So, despite holding patents to perform both *Much Ado* and *Measure*, Davenant decided "to act two old plays under a new title, packaging them as a new product and passing them off as his own enterprise" (372). His objective was, she says, to create a viable play for his newly formed company. The creation of *The Law Against Lovers* had "less to do with Shakespeare, and more to do with providing a vehicle for various forms of entertainment involving song, dance, a popular young actress, music, and novelty" (373). For further commentary, see Cox (no. 155) and Collins (no. 203); for the text, see Davenant (no. 204).

H. Pedagogy.

206a. Andreas, James R. "Writing Down, Speaking Up, Acting Out, and Clowning Around in the Shakespeare Classroom." In *Teaching Shakespeare into the Twenty-first Century*, ed. James E. Davis and Ronald E. Salomone, 25–32. Athens: Ohio Univ. Press, 1997.

Using Dogberry and company as an example, Andreas argues that, through the vulgarity and word-play of the constabulary, students can understand the vanities, pretentions, and cruelties of the social order in Messina—and possibly in their own world. Andreas recommends taking comedy seriously "to catch and secure students' interest, engagement, and even affection" (31).

207. Cookson, Linda, and Bryan Loughrey, eds. *Critical Essays on "Much Ado about Nothing."* London: Longman Group, 1990.

The editors offer a collection of short essays by teachers and theatrical practitioners as models for high-school and college students who seek to develop skills in essay writing using the text of Shakespeare's play as the basis for topics. Each essay is followed by questions that relate the play text to the model essay. The book ends with a practical guide to essay writing, suggestions for further reading, and a style sheet.

208. Hapgood, Robert. "Listening for the Playwright's Voice: Rehearsing through Class Discussion the 'Kill Claudio' Episode." In *Teaching Shakespeare through Performance*, ed. Milla C. Riggio, 145–54. New York: Modern Language Association of America, 1999.

Hapgood describes how he takes a class through the decision-making process of reading each line of the famous scene in order to help students see the complexity of the text and the numerous possibilities in each phase of the scene. After the class has made its decisions, it views the Branagh film to see how some of the challenges are met or evaded—to compare and evaluate readings. The scene is very rich for this purpose, and the description is a model for using this teaching technique with any other scene. For contrasting readings of this scene, see Cox (no. 192) and Steed (no. 202).

209. Skrebels, Paul. "Transhistoricizing *Much Ado about Nothing.*" In *Teaching Shakespeare into the Twenty-first Century*, ed. James E. Davis and Ronald E. Salomone, 81–95. Athens: Ohio Univ. Press, 1997.

Skrebels acknowledges the difficulty of engaging students today in a text that depends on slandering a woman's chastity and the subsequent rejection of her. "The challenge," says Skrebels, "is to transhistoricize the characters of Hero and Claudio... [so] that postmodern readers can accommodate them within their own culture" (87). Skrebels suggests an example comparing Charles, Prince of Wales, and Princess Diana to Claudio and Hero, to focus on scandal and reputation. Skrebels claims that there are many possibilities for analysis in transhistoricization, such as the use of media trickery with camera angles when compared to eavesdropping in the play, and considerations of status, privilege, and celebrity.

See also nos. 76a–78, 286.

I. Collections.

210. Davis, Walter R., ed. *Twentieth Century Interpretations of "Much Ado about Nothing": A Collection of Critical Essays*. Englewood Cliffs, N.J.: Prentice-Hall, 1969.

Part One presents full-length interpretations by John Crick, Francis Fergusson, David Horowitz, Robert G. Hunter, William G. McCollum (no. 174), Graham Storey, Virgil Thomson, and James J. Wey. Part Two presents shorter "viewpoints" by W. H. Auden, Northrop Frye (no. 32), Harold Goddard (no. 49), Dorothy Hockey (no. 183), Walter N. King (no. 186), James A. McPeek, John Palmer, A. P. Rossiter (no. 189), James Smith (no. 190), and Wylie Sypher. The introduction is comprehensive, covering much criticism up to the late sixties. Davis concludes, "Messina is above all a self-absorbed society in which people's concern for appearances argues a self-assurance and smugness that blocks any real sense of connection with the world outside it" (12).

211. Wynne-Davies, Marion, ed. *"Much Ado about Nothing" and "The Taming of the Shrew" New Casebooks.* London: Palgrave, 2001.

For *Much Ado* this collection includes the work of Harry Berger (no. 177), S. P. Cerasano (no. 172), Barbara Everett (no. 181), Penny Gay (no. 68), and Jean Howard (no. 162). Wynne-Davies's introduction explains that both comedies have undergone a sea change in critical opinion, from being viewed as light-hearted and boisterous to being seen as dark and problematic. At the same time, according to Wynne-Davies, critics have become more aware of their own biases and how they affect perceptions of art. So Wynne-Davies has selected essays that are clear about their authors' concerns and relate the plays to their historical contexts.

J. Concordance.

212. Howard-Hill, T. H., ed. *"Much Ado about Nothing": A Concordance to the Text of the First Quarto of 1600.* Oxford: Clarendon Press, 1970.

A separate volume is devoted to each of the twenty-four plays in the Oxford Shakespeare Concordances, which are based on the Oxford Old Spelling Shakespeare. The volume "takes account of every word in the text, and represents their occurrence by frequency counts, line numbers, and reference lines, or a selection of these according to the interest of the particular word" (v).

See also nos. 82–86.

V. TWELFTH NIGHT; OR, WHAT YOU WILL

A. Editions.

213. Donno, Elizabeth Story, ed. *Twelfth Night or What You Will*. The New Cambridge Shakespeare. Cambridge: Cambridge Univ. Press, 1985.

The announced intentions of the New Cambridge Shakespeare are to reflect current critical interests and be attentive "to the realisation of the plays on the stage, and to their social and cultural settings" (v). The text is based on the First Folio. The well-illustrated introduction includes discussions of date (1601) and title, sources, a running commentary on the action and characters, a brief discussion of critical fashions, and an extended theatrical history with a section on recent years by Philip Brockbank, the general editor. An appendix presents detailed comments on the text and the position of the play in the First Folio. The notes provide precise glosses and readings of difficult passages, set scenes, and clarify allusions. This edition is conscientious in its scholarship, but innocent of recent developments in criticism of the play. For her views of recent criticism, see Donno's review article (no. 291).

214. Furness, Horace Howard, ed. *Twelfth Night, or, What You Will*. A New Variorum Edition of Shakespeare. New York: Lippincott, 1901. Repr. New York: Dover Publications, 1964.

In the notes to the text Furness presents variants in major editions from the Second Folio of 1632 to the Cambridge edition of 1891. The editions are identified in the appendix under "Plan of the Work." The footnotes to the text contain readings from the scholarship available to Furness, including his judgments. The appendix deals with various evidence for the date of composition; the sources of the plot: Barnabe Riche's "Apolonius and Silla" in *Riche's Farewell to a Militarie Profession*; a summary of Secchi's *Gl'Inganni* from 1562; a translation of *Gl'Ingannati* from 1531; Bandello's twenty-eighth novella, translated by John Payne; and an excerpt from Sidney's *Arcadia*. Also included are excerpts of criticism from Samuel Pepys in 1661 to the end of the nineteenth century; with comments on the parts of Viola, Malvolio, Feste, and Aguecheek; descriptions of costumes; a time analysis; and translations of "Come away, come away death."

TWELFTH NIGHT 91

215. Lothian, J. N. and T. W. Craik, eds. *Twelfth Night*. The Arden Edition. London: Methuen, 1975.

This edition was begun by Lothian and, after his death, completed by Craik. The text is based on the First Folio. The introduction reviews the possible reasons why *Twelfth Night* is placed between *All's Well* and *Winter's Tale* in the First Folio and the "question of revision," the date (1601) and the title, sources, criticism, Craik's analysis of acts and scenes, and a stage history. An appendix contains pertinent sections of Barnabe Riche's "Apolonius and Silla" from *Riche His Farewell to Militarie Profession*, and another presents the music for the songs. Notes are provided for the characters, to define status and meaning of names; notes to the text, at the bottom of the page, provide glosses, explain allusions, and give contemporary references where helpful.

216. Smith, Bruce R., ed. *"Twelfth Night or What You Will"—Texts and Contexts*. The Bedford Shakespeare Series. New York: St. Martin's, 2001.

The volumes in this series frame a Shakespeare play with a range of written and visual material from contemporary culture: medical texts, sermons, court records, ballads, maps, and much else. The play text is from *The Complete Works of Shakespeare*, edited by David Bevington in 1997, including notes and glosses (no. 1). Cultural materials included are grouped into categories that derive from the play: romance, music, sexuality, clothing and disguise, household economies, Puritan probity, and clowning and laughter. The introduction relates each of the documents to relevant parts of the play. A bibliography includes primary and secondary sources. This is an excellent resource, especially for students seeking primary materials for paper topics.

217. Warren, Roger, and Stanley Wells, eds. *Twelfth Night, or What You Will*. Oxford: Clarendon Press, 1994.

The editors call this a collaborative edition. The text is Wells's for the Oxford *Complete Works*, namely the First Folio. The introduction, written by Warren and revised by Wells, includes the following topics: the occasion of the first performance (1601); the significance of the title; the setting of Illyria; the influence of *Gl'Ingannati* and Emanuel Forde's *Famous History of Parismus*; a comparison of the text to Barnabe Riche's narrative of "Apolonius and Silla"; the treatment of the twins; the various kinds of love represented; the music of the play; the relation of Viola and Olivia, Viola and Orsino, Antonio and Sebastian; the gulling of Malvolio; problems of the intrigue actions; Feste; and the finale. The introduction draws frequent examples from stage history. The notes provide accurate glosses; explain elliptical passages, which are frequent in this play; and provide rich explanations of allusions. An appendix by James Walker presents musical settings.

B. Date and Text.

218. Turner, Robert K. "The Text of *Twelfth Night*." *Shakespeare Quarterly* 26 (1975):128–38.

Turner reviews the evidence supporting and refuting Dover Wilson's theory that the First Folio text of *Twelfth Night* was based on the promptbook with some alterations made for revival of the play. Turner concludes that Wilson's theory is in error, "that F1 *TN* was printed from a scribal copy of Shakespeare's working draft of the play" (137). Turner admits that it is difficult to say why such a transcript was made, "but critics of Shakespeare can, I think, be reasonably confident that the F1 text is two steps away from authorial papers and that the promptbook was not in the line of transmission" (138).

> For the date of *Twelfth Night*, see Donno (no. 213), Furness (no. 214), Lothian and Craik (no. 215), and Warren and Wells (no. 217); Draper (no. 222), Hotson (no. 225), and Osborne (no. 277) also present arguments that are important for dating the play.

C. Influences; Sources; Historical and Intellectual Backgrounds; Topicality.

219. Astington, John. "Malvolio and the Eunuchs: Texts and Revels in *Twelfth Night*." *Shakespeare Survey* 46 (1994): 23–34.

Astington connects the lines about greatness in Maria's letter that dupes Malvolio to Christ's words in *Matthew*: "For there are some Eunuches, which were so borne from their mothers wombe: and there are some Eunuches, which were made Eunuches of men: and there be Eunuches which have made themselves Eunuches for the kingdome of heavens sake" (*Matt.* 19.12). Astington argues that Malvolio's missing of the parallelism is a parody on "the tendency of Puritan interpretation to read ambiguous texts in the direction of a theological programme, or to invoke the will of God to endorse personal predilections" (26). He further connects the ludicrous costume defined in the letter as part of the practice in church festivals, which were noted for their rituals of sexual humiliation and the brutality of bull and bear baiting. Nothing that happens to Malvolio, Astington concludes, lies outside the English Church festival tradition.

220. **Callaghan, Dympna.** "'And all is semblative a woman's part': body politics and *Twelfth Night*." *Textual Practice* 7 (1993): 428–52. Repr. in White (no. 290).

Callaghan explores the paradox of women's exclusion from the English stage to prevent public indecency while *Twelfth Night* represents "female genitals ... at the heart of Malvolio's gulling, the play's most famous scene" (436). According to Callaghan, the public display of Olivia's private parts is humbling for her, as if women performed in plays: "Thus, the very thing that justified women's exclusion from the stage is graphically foregrounded in this play. But the play does not therefore subversively evade the strictures against female bodies on the stage; rather it adds weight to them by presenting the female body in its most biologically essential form—the cunt" (441). Callaghan's purpose is political: "I have insisted on the materiality of women's exclusion from the stage even while examining the representation of her private parts. To do so is to some extent to halt the play of possibilities envisaged by much contemporary cultural analysis of transvestism in order to take a political position which works to open up new space for the purposes of resistance postmodernism." (450) For further commentary on the bawdry, see Scragg (no. 235) and Ungerer (no. 244).

221. **Carroll, William C.** "The Ending of *Twelfth Night* and the Tradition of Metamorphosis." In *Shakespearean Comedy*, ed. Maurice Charney, 49–62. New York: New York Literary Forum, 1980.

Carroll explores the background for Shakespeare's use of the biologically impossible identical twins of different sexes. In Carroll's view, Shakespeare would have found in Ovid a metamorphosis through love of one of a same sex couple to allow their marriage. Such changes, brought about by the gods, appear in Lyly's *Gallathea*, in *Love's Metamorphosis*, and in *The Maydes Metamorphosis* during Shakespeare's time. Carroll claims that Shakespeare depends upon the audience's imagination to see the sameness and difference, inspired by the confusion of Antonio and Feste, and the language about perspective and "what is, is not." The end of the play, Carroll says, emphasizes similarity, but also difference, and the audience is ready to accept both in Viola and Sebastian. For further comments on metamorphosis, see Rackin (no. 60).

222. **Draper, John W.** *The "Twelfth Night" of Shakespeare's Audience.* Stanford: Stanford Univ. Press, 1950.

This work is arranged by characters, and, although it purports to be a study of the cultural responses Shakespeare's audience would have had to their status, it is largely character analysis with some historical background. For example, the chapter on Sir Toby clarifies his status within Olivia's household: he is probably a younger brother of Olivia's father. This work may be useful for readers who wish to understand the socio-economic status of each of the characters. Themes discussed are also emphatically social: "This is Shakespeare's play of social security; and in time of peace, marriage was the chief means by which this prize was gained or lost" (250). There is an appendix on the date of the play, the Elizabethan Christmas season, and an analysis of the time of the action.

223. Elam, Keir. "The Fertile Eunuch: *Twelfth Night*, Early Modern Intercourse, and the Fruits of Castration." *Shakespeare Quarterly* 47 (1996): 1–36.

Elam traces the family tree of the eunuch play (with disguised twins) from Terence's *Eunuchus* and through Ariosto and Bibbiena to Shakespeare, with productive glances at the courtly discourse of Castiglione and Guazzo. He says that *Twelfth Night* does without "the whole *commedia* apparatus of more or less brutal physical engagement and crude sexual bartering" (30). Instead, he claims, "*Twelfth Night* seems to enact a discursivizing ... of the often violent sexual and social intercourse of its antecedents" (30). In this way, says Elam, the play is closer to the "ideological texture of *The Courtier*" than is Italian comedy (30). For another view of Shakespeare's "chastening" his sources, see Hutson (no. 259).

224. Gras, Henk. "*Twelfth Night, Every Man Out of his Humor*, and the Middle Temple Revels of 1597–98." *Modern Language Review* 84 (1989): 545–64.

Gras argues that in *Twelfth Night* Shakespeare uses the very conventions that Jonson held in contempt and ridiculed in *Every Man Out of his Humour* (1599). After citing numerous connections between the two plays, Gras concludes, "The new play [*Twelfth Night*], festive and dreamlike, turns inside out important materials from the first play. It opposes midnight to noonday, romance to satire, lies to truth, love to hatred, natural human weakness to vice, acceptance and surfeit to wounding lashes and purging pills, disguise to perspicuousness and untrussing, far-off Illyria tainted with London Elephants, gallants, and catches, to a London (familiar and near) tainted with Horace, Theophrastus, and the classic dramatic unities." (564) For further comments on Jonson, see Hollander (no. 256).

225. Hotson, Leslie. *The First Night of "Twelfth Night."* London: Rupert Hart-Davis, 1954. Selections repr. in King (no. 287), Palmer (no. 288), and Wells (no. 289).

Taking an historical approach, Hotson claims that the entertainment of Virginio Orsino, Duke of Bracciano, by Elizabeth I on January 6, 1600/1 was the occasion for the first performance of *Twelfth Night*. His case depends on a manuscript memorandum among the papers of the Duke of Northumberland that contains an order to the Master of Revels for a play after supper in Whitehall Palace on January 6, 1601. Hotson cites other confirming documents and an account of the stage Shakespeare would have used for the performance. Although Hotson presents an argument about why the play would have been pleasing to the Queen and the Duke, the portraits of a love-sick Orsino and narcissistic Olivia have not persuaded other critics that the play would have appealed to the audience. The haste with which Shakespeare would have had to work to mount the production has been another barrier to adoption of the hypothesis.

226. Hunt, Maurice. "Malvolio, Viola, and the Question of Instrumentality: Defining Providence in *Twelfth Night*." *Studies in Philology* 90 (1993): 277–97.

According to Hunt, Malvolio's conviction that Jove is to be praised for Olivia's love for him caricatures the Puritan "emphasis upon the virtually unmediated involvement of deity in the daily life of the chosen" (284). This attitude accents Malvolio's egotism and contrasts with Viola's trust in nature, the secondary agent of Providence for Richard Hooker and more conservative Protestants. But, Hunt argues, the fact that Shakespeare gives the impression that Viola earns the blessing of grace "fixes Shakespeare on the far liberal left" of protestant doctrinal opinion (293). For further comments on comic providence, see Hartwig (no. 255); for more on Puritan reading of texts, see Astington (no. 219).

227. Hunt, Maurice. "*Twelfth Night* and the Annunciation." *Papers on Language and Literature* 25 (1989): 264–71.

Hunt detects echoes of the Annunciation scene in Cesario's first interview with Olivia, who is called madonna by Feste. He points out that, like the angel Gabriel, Cesario holds an olive branch, and, like Gabriel's, Cesario's message is "to your ears divinity." Hunt claims that when Cesario declares, "My matter hath no voice, lady, but to your own most pregnant and vouchsafed ear" (3.1.90–91), the allusion emphasizes the fact that Twelfth Night was a time for consecration of virgins and also parodies the Petrarchan discourse of Orsino and Cesario. The contrast between the madonna Olivia and the Madonna accents Olivia's egotism, but the comparison prepares us, according to Hunt, for Olivia's growth toward marriage.

228. Hurworth, Angela. "Gulls, Cony-Catchers and Cozeners: *Twelfth Night* and the Elizabethan Underworld." *Shakespeare Survey* 52 (1999): 120–32.

Hurworth compares "the representation of gulling in *Twelfth Night* with the narratives of underworld literature where such deception, known as cony-catching, cozenage or gulling, receives its fullest treatment" (121). Hurworth sees Maria's gulling Sir Toby as harmless, and Sir Toby's gulling of Sir Andrew as typical of the gallant and his gull in the pamphlets. But the gulling of Malvolio is very complex: "In *Twelfth Night* the plot to gull Malvolio introduces a theatrical *mise en abyme*, the intradramatic doubling of all aspects of performance. It is an additional layer of reflexivity in a play whose plot turns upon the confusion engendered by the existence of twins, where narcissism creates its own double[s], and where disguise inverts notions of sameness and difference" (129). For Hurworth, the gulling exposes Malvolio as an ambitious hypocrite, but it turns cruel: "The 'sportful malice' turns its perpetrators into sadistic persecutors in its latter stages, and demonstrates that gulling may unleash evil impulses in apparently good-natured characters" (131). For additional comments on doubles, see Fineman (no. 251); for more on cony-catchers, see Scragg (no. 235); for the cruel gulling, see Berry (no. 247).

229. Ko, Yu Jin. "The Comic Close of *Twelfth Night* and Viola's *Noli me tangere*." *Shakespeare Quarterly* 48 (1997): 391–405.

Ko reads Viola's command to Sebastian not to embrace her until she is dressed as a woman through Christ's words to Mary Magdalene. "When Shakespeare has Viola reject Sebastian's approach in the final scene, we in the audience experience not only the pain of deferral but its deep pleasure as well. As the moment lingers, the characters become icons in a larger drama that shares with religious drama a vision of secular desire but which contains no promise of transcendent fulfillment." (398)

230. Lamb, Mary Ellen. "Ovid's *Metamorphoses* and Shakespeare's *Twelfth Night*." In *Shakespearean Comedy*, ed. Maurice Charney, 63–78. New York: New York Literary Forum, 1980.

Lamb sees contradictory interpretations of Ovid's tales: they were allegorical representations of the human soul, and they were playful, ambiguous, erotic narratives. The allusions to *The Metamorphoses* in *Twelfth Night* suggest, according to Lamb, how Viola and Sebastian rescue Orsino and Olivia from inner stagnation. Lamb contends that Viola's and Feste's role-playing confirms the similarity between Ovid's Rome and Shakespeare's Illyria.

231. Lamb, Mary Ellen. "Tracing a Heterosexual Erotics of Service, and the Autobiographical Writings of Thomas Whythorne and Anne Clifford." *Criticism* 40 (1998): 1–25.

Lamb uses the diaries of Wythorne, a servant in several female-headed households of Shakespeare's contemporaries, and Clifford, a noblewoman, to contextualize the Malvolio action in *Twelfth Night*: the diaries reveal the frequent dependence of widows or isolated wives on upper servants, leading them to form relationships that were close and sometimes sexual. The play, Lamb asserts, raises and then dispels anxieties about servants as a result of the decline of the ideology of service. Lamb believes that marriage removes the threat of the Orsino-Cesario-Olivia relations, and Malvolio's ambition earns a self-imposed exile. She claims that Feste illustrates the predicament of a servant caught between two economic systems—a money economy and an apparently insufficient system of service. For further comments on servants, see Malcolmson (no. 233), Jardine (no. 260), and Slights (no. 267).

232. Lewalski, Barbara K. "Thematic Patterns in *Twelfth Night*." *Shakespeare Studies* 1 (1965): 168–81.

Lewalski argues that *Twelfth Night* may be read in accordance with the Christmas season, which is ended by the Feast of the Epiphany: "The word is made flesh and continues to dwell among us" (169). In this interpretation, Illyria is idyllic, a place of Good Will, which is still much in need of restoration with Malvolio an enemy of love and merrymaking, Toby and company dedicated to disorder, Olivia given to melancholy and madness, and Orsino doting on love melancholy. Lewalski sees the wit of Maria and the the spirit of Feste as internal cures, but the twins coming from the outside are necessary to bring "Peace that is the special promise of the season" (174). For Lewalski, Viola is "the embodiment of selfless love" (175), and Sebastian restores order to society in his betrothal to Olivia and his punishment of Toby and Andrew. According to Lewalski, Feste's final song reminds the audience that Illyria is a promise far from the real world.

233. Malcolmson, Cristina. "'What You Will': Social Mobility and Gender in *Twelfth Night*." *The Matter of Difference: Materialist Feminist Criticism of Shakespeare*, ed. Valerie Wayne, 29–57. Ithaca: Cornell Univ. Press, 1991. Repr. in White, no. 290.

Malcolmson explores the relation of class (social status) to gender in *Twelfth Night*. Both men and women, she says, improve their lot through the marriage market, but women are allowed to violate social boundaries more successfully than men. "*Twelfth Night* sets free a fluidity between the roles of man and woman, and master and servant in the case of Viola and Maria, but limits it severely and abruptly in the case of Malvolio" (36). Malcolmson argues that Malvolio's dream of marrying Olivia is no more disruptive than hers of marrying the gentleman-servant Cesario. She claims Malvolio's defect is that his desire is for status and power, not love. "This allows the play to question quite fully the traditional ideology that those who rule are mentally or morally superior to those who are ruled, but it holds such questioning in check through the ideal of marriage" (39). For further comments on servants and women, see Lamb (no. 231) and Jardine (no. 260).

234. Palmer, D. J. "*Twelfth Night* and the Myth of Echo and Narcissus." *Shakespeare Survey* 32 (1979): 73–78.

Palmer relates the self-engrossment and vanity of Orsino, Olivia, and Malvolio to Ovid's account of the myth of Narcissus. He argues that Viola has the role of Echo in her concealment of unrequited love. Palmer speculates that Viola's postponement of final clarification of Sebastian's identity may lie in her "distrust of appearances in the uncertain and unstable world of Illyria" (78). This article has been highly influential. For further comments about this myth and identity, see Carroll (no. 221), Ko (no. 229), Lamb (no. 230), and Taylor (no. 238).

235. Scragg, Leah. "'Her C's, Her U's, and Her T's: Why That?' A New Reply for Sir Andrew Aguecheek." *Review of English Studies* 42 (1991): 1–16.

Scragg puts a further connotation on the already bawdy implications of the letters Malvolio selects from the letter he reads in 2.5 of *Twelfth Night* to convince himself that it is written in Olivia's script. Scragg notices that after laughing at "the incongruity of 'cut' and 'pee' in the mouth of the steward, members of the audience are encouraged [by Sir Andrew's repetition of the letters] to visualize 'cut-P——'" or cutpurse (14). Scragg points out that early modern theatres were gathering places for pickpockets, whose techniques were amply described in the cony-catching pamphlets and the city comedies of Shakespeare's contemporaries. For further implications of this bawdry see Callaghan (no. 220) and Ungerer (no. 244); for more on cony-catching, see Hurworth (no. 228).

236. Siegel, Paul N. "Malvolio: Comic Puritan Automaton." In *Shakespearean Comedy*, ed. Maurice Charney, 217–30. New York: New York Literary Forum, 1980.

Siegel investigates the application of *Puritan* to Malvolio and finds that stock epithets for Puritans are routinely applied to the steward by Sir Toby, Sir Andrew, and Maria. Siegel claims that Malvolio behaves very much like a Puritan in his reading of the letter and his wearing cross garters and that, far from being a tragic figure, Malvolio remains a comic automaton in the Bergsonian sense. For differing views of Malvolio's gulling, see Hurworth (no. 228), Berry (no. 247), Hunter (no. 257), and Levin (no. 263).

237. Smith, Peter J. "M. O. A. I. 'What should that alphabetical position portend?' An Answer to the Metamorphic Malvolio." *Renaissance Quarterly* 51 (1998): 199–224.

Smith attempts to solve the puzzle presented by the statement in Maria's letter, "M. O. A. I. doth sway my life." Whether one is persuaded by Smith's argument that the letters refer to John Harington's *Metamorphosis of AIAX*, a bawdy work published in 1596, Smith's summaries of the many other scholars' attempts to solve the puzzle are informative. For further comments about M. O. A. I., see Lewis (no. 243) and Osborne (no. 277).

238. Taylor, A. B. "Shakespeare Rewriting Ovid: Olivia's Interview with Viola and the Narcissus Myth." *Shakespeare Survey* 50 (1997): 81–89.

Taylor compares Olivia at the beginning of *Twelfth Night* to Narcissus at the moment before he sees his image in the pool. "The interview where passion first enters the life of Shakespeare's own beautiful young recluse, throwing her into confusion and inflaming her, too, with ardent desire for a non-existent 'boy,' begins with a variation of Ovid's motif and the Narcissus image" (83). According to Taylor, the comparison of Olivia's beauty to a picture and the catalogue of her features are present in Ovid; Cesario becomes Echo as s/he repeats Orsino's words and projects her own frustrated love for Orsino. Taylor claims that Malvolio's self-love is a contrast to that of Orsino and Olivia. As they move from darkness to sunlight, Malvolio "moves from shadow into darkness, from confusion into madness" (88). According to Taylor, Malvolio is a powerful warning against what Orsino and Olivia have escaped. For further comments on Ovid, see Carroll (no. 221), Lamb (no. 230), and Palmer (no. 234).

239. Wheeler, Richard P. "Deaths in the Family: The Loss of a Son and the Rise of Shakespearean Comedy." *Shakespeare Quarterly* 51 (2000): 127–53.

Wheeler sees the fantasy of restoration of Shakespeare's dead son Hamnet (a male twin) in *As You Like It* and *The Merchant of Venice*, but most intensely in *Twelfth Night*, where Viola is "a twin who appears to have survived the death of her brother. *Twelfth Night* puts right at the center of the action a situation structurally analogous to the death of Hamnet and the survival of Judith in the Shakespeare family. And that action will bring the dead son and brother back." (147) Wheeler comments on the immersion of characters in melancholy and mourning, the undertow of sadness in *Twelfth Night*, and the moving reunion of brother and sister. For further comments on loss and return, see Fineman (no. 251) and Freedman (no. 252).

D. Language and Linguistics.

240. Booth, Stephen. *Precious Nonsense: The Gettysburg Address, Ben Jonson's Epitaphs on his Children, and "Twelfth Night."* Berkeley: Univ. of California Press, 1998.

Twelfth Night is for Booth the longest and most telling example of an exploration of nonsense in literature that he has been presenting for years. Booth cites a number of examples of the language of *Twelfth Night* that do not make sense to him, beginning with Orsino's opening speech and moving to many of Sir Toby's lines, which Booth believes provoke laughter because they sound as if they should. Booth dwells on the propriety and impropriety of Fabian's comment on the action, and the closure and lack of closure at the end of the play. Booth's manner gives the effect of the *tour de force*, but he has captured an important quality of the play that other readers may experience but do not articulate. For further comments on nonsense in this play, see Hartman (no. 242).

241. Eagleton, Terence. "Language and Reality in *Twelfth Night*." *Critical Quarterly* 9 (1967): 217–28.

Eagleton gives several examples of the way the play's language "sucks life from real human existence" and thereby controls life (218). He observes, "The illusory, interchangeable quality of language in the play, its capacity to absorb and regulate the substance of human reality, has a direct parallel in the action of the drama itself: in the illusions, switchings and mistakes involved in the adoption of human roles" (221). For Eagleton, the clown is the essence of this effect because linguistic liberty is the main element of his role. "The Clown's sanity—his reality—springs from the fact that he fulfills a settled role consistently, and it is the lack of such consistency in the play as a whole which suggests that illusion and insanity are general conditions" (227–28).

242. Hartman, Geoffrey H. "Shakespeare's Poetical Character in *Twelfth Night*." In *Shakespeare and the Question of Theory*, ed. Patricia Parker and Geoffrey Hartman, 37–53. New York and London: Routledge, 1985. Repr. in White (no. 290).

For Hartman, *Twelfth Night* exemplifies the thesis that "the locus of the dramatic action [is] the effect of language on character" (38). Hartman observes that *Twelfth Night* devotes an extraordinary amount of time to the clowning of minor characters and to puns and anagrams. To the question, "what filling (fulfilling) is in this fooling, the best reply might be that, in literature, everything aspires to the condition of language, to the gift of tongues; that the spirit—wanton as it may be—of language overrides such questions, including those of character and identity" (48). The arbitrariness of language accounts, for Hartman, for the differences among interpretations. For more about fooling in this play, see Booth (no. 240).

243. Lewis, Cynthia. " 'A Fustian Riddle'? Anagrammatic Names in *Twelfth Night*." *English Language Notes* 22 (1985): 32–37.

Lewis observes that several of the names in the play are *near* anagrams for one another. She also notes that Malvolio, whose name echoes those of Viola and Olivia, resists the final community of lovers entirely, yet he has been tricked by jumping to conclusions about M. O. A. I. The audience, Lewis cautions, should not seek solutions to the anagrams: "If we seek meaning in them, like Puritans scanning the Bible for encoded assurance of their election, we seek foolishly" (37). For further comments about M. O. A. I., see Smith (no. 237) and Osborne (no. 277).

244. Ungerer, Gustav. " 'My Lady's A Catayan, We Are Politicians, Malvolio's a Peg-a-Ramsie.' " *Shakespeare Survey* 32 (1979): 85–104.

Ungerer argues that Sir Toby is not uttering confused, drunken language, but is quite in control of his epithets. "Catayan," according to Ungerer, is far from a term of abuse, but implies that Olivia, like Queen Elizabeth and the Countess of Pembroke, was an investor (and therefore rich enough to be so) in the search for a Northwest passage to Cathay. In addition, Ungerer says, "Malvolio's identification as a 'Peg-a-Ramsie' and a 'Iezabel' is obviously meant to expose the steward's jealous nature and lascivious disposition" (97). Ungerer relates this characterization to Malvolio's references to bawdy songs and his obscenities with reference to Olivia's handwriting. For further comments about bawdry, see Callaghan (no. 220) and Scragg (no. 235).

245. Yearling, Elizabeth M. "Language, Theme, and Character in *Twelfth Night*." *Shakespeare Survey* 35 (1982): 79–86.

Yearling analyzes the way in which characters' diction and syntax reveal their inner beings. For Yearling, Feste is the self-confessed corrupter of words. Viola uses the greatest variety of discourses: "Her vocabulary ranges from courtly compliment to rude jargon (1.5.205). But her variousness is not just verbal: her nature is to deal confidently with sudden changes. And the assumed registers, coupled often with sincere feelings, capture the blend of truth and illusion which Viola represents." (81) According to Yearling, Orsino uses long sentences, pompous diction, and sustained images; Sir Toby invents long words and mixes mannered syntax with colloquial vocabulary; and Olivia interrupts her musings about time, beauty, and love with simple, direct questions that imply action and command. Yearling argues that Malvolio's language is constrained and pompous: "He introduces fewer new words than either Orsino or Sir Toby, but his mouth is full of pompous phrases and long words without the poetry of Orsino or the colloquialism of Sir Toby" (83).

See also nos. 39–41, 140.

E. Criticism.

246. Anderson, Linda. *A Kind of Wild Justice: Revenge in Shakespeare's Comedies.* Newark: Univ. of Delaware Press, 1987.

Anderson presents an extended reading of the Malvolio plot in *Twelfth Night* as a revenge action. It is especially humiliating, she contends, for the ambitious Malvolio to be gulled by a waiting woman, a servant, a clown, a coxcomb, and a drunkard.

247. Berry, Ralph. "*Twelfth Night*: The Experience of the Audience." *Shakespeare Survey* 34 (1981): 111–19.

Berry contends that *Twelfth Night* is less festive than most critics think. He finds Sir Toby less appealing than usually portrayed because he is exploitative of both his niece and Sir Andrew. For Berry, Maria is marked by "a willingness to stir up trouble for others" (114). These defects, combined with Feste's dark side, lead them to take the joke on Malvolio too far, and the audience, according to Berry, becomes queasy about the obvious victim. "I surmise that the ultimate effect of *Twelfth Night* is to make the audience ashamed of itself" (119). Whether one accepts Berry's major premise or does not, his reading of Malvolio's behavior and language in the cell is the most sensitive in commentary on the play. For further comment on the gulling, see Hurworth (no. 228).

248. Codden, Karin S. "'Slander in an Allow'd Fool': *Twelfth Night's* Crisis of the Aristocracy." *Studies in English Literature 1500–1900* 33 (1993): 309–23.

Codden argues that *Twelfth Night* in effect has it both ways: it mocks the aristocratic indulgence of holiday and makes clear the instability of rank and order. For Codden, Feste tests the limits of licensed foolery with unruliness and takes dark glances at frustrated desire and the historical world outside the gates. "The time of carefree, aristocratic festivity is gone, and between nostalgia for an idealized past and uncertainty about the historical time beyond holiday is the tenuous and ironical celebration of the present" (317). Codden concludes that the closing song "marks the end of holiday time and takes the play back into history, into materiality" (322–23). For further comment on the aristocracy, see Goddard (no. 49), Wilcher (no. 65), Malcolmson (no. 233), and Summers (no. 268).

249. Crewe, Jonathan. "In the Field of Dreams: Transvestism in *Twelfth Night* and *The Crying Game*." *Representations* 50 (1995): 101–21.

In the part of this essay devoted to *Twelfth Night*, Crewe gives a detailed account of the multiple desires and love objects released in the play by the transvestite intermediary, especially in relation to the marriage plot. "The play's solution, which establishes a 'new' gender equity by dividing power and desire between the principals, depends on the production of another copy of Viola/Cesario. Each principal thereby gains some of what he or she wills and still avoids the fully exogamous other, while the social resolution of the androgyne into its male and female parts with the arrival of Sebastian promises to disambiguate the play's gendered subjects and objects of desire, though not without a large residue of bigendered and bisexual subjectivity." (111–12)

250. Everett, Barbara. "Or What You Will." *Essays in Criticism* 35 (1985): 294–314. Repr. in White (no. 290).

Everett tries to define the true seriousness of "the best and last of Shakespeare's comedies" (294). She notes that the setting is timeless at first, the plot an amalgam of devices Shakespeare used before, and that the resolution depends on an impossibility—boy-girl identical twins. She notes, too, that the play's language is "a romantic language whose law is a sardonic and charming evasion of the restraints of social reality" (299–300). In her view, all characters—high and low—are playing at life. Even Malvolio has a fantasy about "my some rich jewel." *Twelfth Night*, for Everett, "catches up into itself a great complex of human reactions to all our lighter, but still serious, attempts to shape time, to control our lives" (303). For Everett, almost all characters are humiliated, with the possible exception of Feste, and this helps the audience see the characters' need for fulfillment in love. She concludes, "There is enough in his handling of the twinship of brother and sister, in itself a romantic myth, an impossibility in nature, to make us see it as perhaps the play's image of the pursuit of a kind of wholeness beyond expression and perhaps beyond possibility" (312-13). For further comment on the twins, see Carroll (no. 221), Fineman (no. 251), and Freedman (no. 252).

251. Fineman, Joel. "Fratricide and Cuckoldry: Shakespeare's Doubles." In *Representing Shakespeare: New Psychoanalytic Essays*, ed. Murray M. Schwartz and Coppélia Kahn, 70–109. Baltimore: Johns Hopkins Univ. Press, 1980.

Fineman explores the themes of fratricide, doubling, and cuckoldry in *Hamlet*, *As You Like It*, and *Twelfth Night*. He argues that both *As You Like It* and *Twelfth Night* develop "a dialectic of Differences rooted in the temporary dissolution of sex difference" (83). Both plays, he says, compare the relative infidelities of men and women to define sexual difference. Fineman asserts that *Twelfth Night* reassures the audience that sexual difference survives because the difference between brother and sister (doubles) is crucial. Fineman generalizes, "The dialectic of Difference and no Difference contained by the original fratricide structure is transferred by Shakespeare to another formula of mirroring reciprocity, to themes of women and their 'frailty,' to a kind of masculine misogyny that finds in the ambiguity of women its own self-divided self-consciousness, its own vulnerability, its mortality" (89). For further comments on doubles, see Hurworth (no. 228); for comments on twins, see Carroll (no. 221); for comments about loss, see Wheeler (no. 239) and Freedman (no. 252).

252. Freedman, Barbara. "Naming Loss: Mourning and Representation in *Twelfth Night*." In *Staging the Gaze: Postmodernism, Psychoanalysis, and Shakespearean Comedy*, 192–235. Ithaca: Cornell Univ. Press, 1991.

Freedman uses Lacanian psychoanalysis, Renaissance optics, postmodern literary theory, and Shakespeare's comedies to make a blend of theories, in which no one is master or primary text. "This model of reading is essentially *theatrical* insofar as it works at the intersection of various theories in order to subvert the place of one's look" (5). Freedman reads *Twelfth Night* as the end of the romantic comedies, a play that deals with loss and death, but denies both through constant repetition and recapitulation of the previous eleven comedies, as well as of its own elements, as in identical twins. For Freedman, the characters are defined by how they deal with abandonment, loss, disillusion, or rejection. Freedman emphasizes the price Viola pays for bringing vitality to others. "Viola deals with loss through near-morbid over-identification, champions mutuality while withholding her own feelings, and develops clarity of vision through visual trickery and disguise" (205). The play's ambiguity and refusal to be clear are part of its value, according to Freedman: "By leaving itself unfinished, by holding back what *it* will, the play derives depth and individuality, emphasizes its separateness from us, and questions our need to find completion in it" (206). For further comments about loss, see Wheeler (no. 239) and Fineman (no. 251).

253. Greenblatt, Stephen. "Fiction and Friction." In *Shakespearean Negotiations: The Circulation of Social Energy in Renaissance England*, 66–93. Berkeley: Univ. of California Press, 1988. Repr. in White (no. 290).

Greenblatt sees a swerving from nature, in the form of illicit sexuality, as one of *Twelfth Night*'s central structural principles, linking the characters' private motivations with the larger social order. Greenblatt historicizes the play's investigation of sexual nature through analysis of other discourses of the body, in which male and female sexual organs are mirror images. He argues that, according to this model, the male/female twins are condensed into the single, but double sexed figure of Cesario. The essence of Shakespearean comedy, for Greenblatt, is the representation of the emergence of identity through the experience of erotic heat. He asserts that, although the consummations of desire are heterosexual, the energy and confusions of Shakespearean comedy depend upon the mobility of desire and the blurring of sexual identities. For him, this energy is connected to the theatre, where male actors perform female parts.

254. Greif, Karen. "Plays and Playing in *Twelfth Night*." *Shakespeare Survey* 34 (1981): 121–30. Repr. in Wells (no. 289).

Greif contrasts the happy outcome of the main action with the unhappy result in the subplot: "While Viola's masquerade serves to redeem Orsino and Olivia from their romantic fantasies and ends in happiness with the final love-matches, the more negative aspects of deception are exposed in the trick played against Malvolio, which leads only to humiliation and deeper isolation" (121). Greif emphasizes the fluidity of identity that is necessary to make the main plot work, while the subplot depends upon characters' being fixed in their roles. For Greif, Malvolio, Sir Toby,

Maria, and Sir Andrew are all ignorant of their own foibles and so "the spectators are in their own ways as much drowned in excesses of folly and imagination as their gull" (127).

255. Hartwig, Joan. "Feste's 'Whirligig' and the Comic Providence of *Twelfth Night*." *ELH* 40 (1973): 501-13.

Hartwig draws a contrast between the providence (by many names characters give it) that rules individual will in the main plot and the parodic human manipulation that governs the subplot. "The foibles of the romantics in Illyria are seen in their reduced terms through Sir Toby, Maria, and Sir Andrew, but the limitations of the parodic characters also heighten by contrast the expansive and expanding world of the play. Love, not revenge, is celebrated." (510) For Hartwig, the harshness of the revenge action keeps the golden time at the end from being complete: "Feste's manipulation of Malvolio resembles the playwright's manipulation of his audience's will, but in such a reduced way that we cannot avoid seeing the difference between merely human revenge and the larger benevolence that controls the play's design" (513). For further comments on providence, see Hunt (no. 226).

256. Hollander, John. "*Twelfth Night* and the Morality of Indulgence." *Sewanee Review* 68 (1959): 220-38. Repr. in King (no. 287) and Palmer (no. 288).

Hollander claims that in *Twelfth Night* Shakespeare wrote a moral comedy diametrically opposed to the humors comedy of Ben Jonson. Instead of a static, deterministic humor regulating human psychology as in Jonson, Shakespeare created a kinetic, governing appetite, according to Hollander, and therefore the play's action is a revel, in which love, eating, and music are the chief components. Hollander associates the play's characters with their indulged appetites: Orsino for romantic love, Olivia for excessive grief, Feste for revelry, and Malvolio for self-love; the play's action is the killing off of excessive appetite through indulgence, leading to a rebirth of the unencumbered self. For Hollander, Feste's final song recapitulates the images of water, elements, and humors that reflect the fluidity of revelling. For further comment on Jonson, see Gras (no. 224).

257. Hunter, G. K. "Plot and Subplot in *Twelfth Night*." In *Shakespeare: The Later Comedies*, 43-55. London: Longmans Green, 1962. Selection repr. in King (no. 287).

For Hunter, Malvolio's ambition is a variant of the self-indulgent obsessions of Olivia and Orsino. The concealed nature of Malvolio's aspiration echoes the hidden truths of the major characters, including Viola. For Hunter the characters do not grow in understanding, but the plot simply moves them to desirable—and socially acceptable—relationships. Because of the prominence of Malvolio at the end of the action, Hunter argues, the principal effect of the denouement is a sense of release from the complexity and concealment of the action. For further comments on plot and subplot, see Taylor (no. 238) and Levin (no. 263).

258. **Huston, J. Dennis.** " 'When I Came to Man's Estate': *Twelfth Night* and Problems of Identity." *Modern Language Quarterly* 33 (1972): 274–88.

Huston reads *Twelfth Night* as a bittersweet play in which the unresolved identity problems of the major characters "qualify the happiness of the resolution" (288). According to Huston, Viola adopts her disguise to try out the freedom of being male, taking a psychic holiday before the commitments of womanhood. But Malvolio's imprisonment echoes, to Huston, the confinement of Olivia and Orsino, both of whom act childishly and impulsively. "In a world so marked by constriction, marriage may also appear another form of imprisonment, particularly when it is entered upon in such haste and for such foolish reasons" (288).

259. **Hutson, Lorna.** "On Not Being Deceived: Rhetoric and the Body in *Twelfth Night*." *Texas Studies in Literature and Language* 38 (1996): 140–74.

Hutson provides a spirited reply to the many critics who see the body and sexuality at the center of *Twelfth Night*. Her counterargument is that Shakespeare's Terentian five-act comedic plot is concerned with "men's discursive ability to improvise social credit, or credibility" (147). Hutson emphasizes the fact that the nineteenth-century women writers about Shakespeare found the play chaste and that what concerns much of the play is social status, not gender. Shakespeare, she adds, routinely "chastens" material derived from Italian and Roman sources. Emphasizing questions of social status, she concludes by comparing *Twelfth Night* to Chapman's *Gentleman Usher* and to the contemporary Duchess of Suffolk's marriage to her gentleman usher. For further comments on social status, see Lamb (no. 231), Malcolmson (no. 233), and Jardine (no. 260); for "chastening" sources, see Elam (no. 223).

260. **Jardine, Lisa.** "Twins and travesties: Gender, dependency and sexual availability in *Twelfth Night*." In *Erotic Politics: Desire on the Renaissance Stage*, ed. Susan Zimmerman, 22–38. London: Routledge, 1992.

Taking the household as the patriarchal unit, Jardine argues that sexual availability and economic dependency were equivalent for both sexes in relation to those above their station. She shows how both Viola and Sebastian seek service in Orsino's household and that Sebastian, when mistaken for Cesario, believes that Olivia will take him into her service. Jardine concludes, "When Orsino takes the hand of Cesario, at the close of the play, and claims her as his sexual partner, he does no more than confirm the terms of his original engagement with his 'young gentleman'" (33). Jardine believes that Olivia's come-uppance for usurping male prerogatives is mistaking Cesario for her mate, which is "most socially and sexually transgressive" (33). For further comments on social status, see Lamb (no. 231), Malcolmson (no. 233), and Hutson (no. 259).

261. Jenkins, Harold. "Shakespeare's *Twelfth Night*." *Shakespeare Newsletter*. Extra Issue 1997, 13–18. First published as a Rice Institute Pamphlet 45 (1959): 19–42. Selections repr. in Muir (no. 81) and Wells (no. 289).

Jenkins believes that Orsino and Olivia are eventually educated by their experiences with Viola/Cesario, unlike Malvolio, who remains fixed in his self-love. Jenkins carefully analyzes the two important scenes that make growth possible: the meeting of the page and the lady (1.5) and the conversations of the page and the Duke about love (2.4). "It is her role to draw Orsino and Olivia from their insubstantial passions and win them to reality" (17). Both Olivia and Orsino are made to look absurd, but that is part of the process: "Olivia, who self-confessedly abandons reason, and Orsino, who avidly gives his mind to all the shapes of fancy, are permitted to pass through whatever folly there may be in this to greater illumination" (18).

262. Kerrigan, John. "Secrecy and Gossip in *Twelfth Night*." *Shakespeare Survey* 50 (1997): 65–80.

Kerrigan applies a combination of anthropological observation and the imperatives of the courtesy books to the conduct of Cesario, Malvolio, Sir Toby, and Sir Andrew. Throughout the play Kerrigan notes the petty jealousies among the serving people in both houses, directed chiefly at Cesario and Malvolio, both of whom are rightly favored by their master/mistress. Kerrigan also notes the frequent temptations of Cesario to reveal his/her identity, and the discretion that Viola has learned as a gentle woman. Of Malvolio's disguise, he says, "To assume yellow stockings and be cross-gartered puts Malvolio's discretion on display, without abolishing it, because the new garb allows him, as he thinks, to share a secret with Olivia, to signal an ambition and grasp of courtly intrigue ... which she will understand and the drinkers and babblers will not" (77). At the end Orsino and Olivia are the characters concerned about Malvolio, Kerrigan points out, and the comedy cannot end until the Captain held in "durance" by Malvolio is released with Viola's female clothes.

263. Levin, Harry. "The Underplot of *Twelfth Night*." In *Shakespeare and the Revolution of the Times*, 131–42. New York: Oxford Univ. Press, 1976. Repr. in Wells (no. 289).

Levin considers the function of the minor characters in *Twelfth Night*: Toby, Maria, Andrew, and primarily Malvolio. The history of response to the play shows that Malvolio has always been judged more important than the length of his part suggests. Levin analyzes how the underplot satirizes the romantic pretensions of the characters in the main plot. A sycophant, social climber, and snob, Malvolio is punished according to folklore—casting a scapegoat into darkness, says Levin. In his view, the baiting of Malvolio is not sadistic, but an affirmation of life, and Shakespeare commits himself to the wisdom of folly and the foolishness of conventional wisdom. For further comment on Malvolio, see Siegel (236), Berry (no. 247), and Hunter (no. 257).

264. Moglen, Helene. "Disguise and Development: the Self and Society in *Twelfth Night*." *Literature and Psychology* 23 (1973): 13–20.

Moglen uses Freud's theories of psychosexual development to read major characters in *Twelfth Night*. She sees Orsino and Olivia emerging from childish narcissism in which both have been locked, only to be liberated by Viola through transitional homoerotic relationships: "Sexual roles are explored and defined, conflicts are resolved and Viola is the medium and the measure" (15). The experimental assumption of roles allows characters, Moglen says, to achieve a "healthful state of love and self-definition" (18). For Moglen, Sebastian is allowed a transitional relationship to Antonio before accepting marriage to Olivia. But, Moglen says, the subplot proceeds on a social, rather than a developmental level because Malvolio's egotism deprives him of the self-knowledge necessary for development.

265. Pequigney, Joseph. "The Two Antonios and Same-Sex Love in *Twelfth Night* and *The Merchant of Venice*." *English Language Review* 22 (1992): 201–21.

Pequigney explores the Antonio-Sebastian relationship in *Twelfth Night* in detail and concludes that his relationship to Antonio initiates Sebastian into interpersonal sexuality, that Sebastian is bisexual, and his relations with Antonio prepare him for his relationship with Olivia: "The reason for

Antonio's portrayal as homosexual is that a liaison with him opens space for Sebastian in the diverse bisexual fictions that make up *Twelfth Night*" (210). In contrast, Pequigney asserts, the relationship between Antonio and Bassanio is amicable, rather than sexual. Yet in Pequigney's reading, both Antonios are included in the loving community at the end of the plays. In *Merchant* Antonio is the agent of reconciliation between Portia and Bassanio, and in *Twelfth Night* Sebastian's reconciliation with his friend does not imply rejection because of the marriage to Olivia. For further comments about male bonds, see Adelman (no. 42), Traub (no. 62), and Osborne (no. 276).

266. Salingar, Leo G. "The Design of *Twelfth Night*." *Shakespeare Quarterly* 9 (1958): 117–39. Selections repr. in King (no. 287) and Wells (no. 289).

Salingar argues that *Twelfth Night* combines effects in a delicate balance between irony and sentiment. He claims that Shakespeare creates this balance by giving prominence to the subplot of misrule in Olivia's household. Salinger emphasizes the saturnalian spirit which he sees pervading the play, as the four main characters seem to reverse their desires by the end. For Salingar, Shakespeare makes their actions spring from the irrational nature of love and accents this theme with the farcical subplot. The romance elements of the main plot move *Twelfth Night* away from the comedy of intrigue to what Salingar calls the triumph of natural love. This essay has been very influential on subsequent criticism.

267. Slights, Camille. "The Principle of Recompense in *Twelfth Night*." *Modern Language Review* 77 (1982): 537–46.

Slights reads *Twelfth Night* through the anthropological principle that, although humans may long for inviolable autonomy, social order requires mutuality based on exchange—of money, of service, of love. "In *Twelfth Night*," Slights argues, "money symbolizes not love so much as a broader engagement with the real and imperfect world" (543). Furthermore, all the major characters dream of self-sufficiency, "but have been forced, by circumstances and by their own needs and desires, into relationships where they become aware of their obligations to and dependence on others" (545). In the separation of Cesario into Sebastian and Viola, Slights sees Levi-Strauss's theory that reciprocity balances the incest prohibition by holding the group together, while the twins rescue the Illyrians from their internal conflicts. For further comments on service, see Lamb (no. 231) and Jardine (no. 260); for another view of mutuality, see Novy (no. 59).

268. Summers, Joseph H. "The Masks of *Twelfth Night*." In *Shakespeare:*

Modern Essays in Criticism, ed. Leonard F. Dean, 134–43. Oxford: Oxford Univ. Press, 1967. Selections repr. in King (no. 287) and Palmer (no. 288).

Summers holds that all the characters in the play wear masks that conceal their identities or at least their motives, masks in which they are masters as well as butts of the audience's laughter. Summers is almost alone among critics in believing that Viola "plays her role with undisguised enjoyment" (138). According to Summers, Sebastian's mask is thrust upon him by Viola's. For Summers, Malvolio "is ridiculous in his arrogance to the end, and his threatened revenge, now that he is powerless to effect it, sustains the comedy and the characterization and prevents the obtrusion of destructive pathos" (142). Feste is the one professional masker, but Summers sees him as old and grumpy, restless in a role he cannot abandon. He "finally reminds us of the limitations and the costs of the romantic vision of happiness with which we have been seduced" (142). For further comments on Feste, see Wilcher (no. 65), Codden (no. 248), and Greif (no. 274).

269. **Warren, Roger.** "'Smiling at Grief': Some Techniques of Comedy in *Twelfth Night* and *Cosi Fan Tutte*." *Shakespeare Survey* 32 (1979): 79–84.

Warren argues that Shakespeare and Mozart achieve a similar effect using differing art forms: "Both works present, essentially, a survey of lovers' behaviour—their extravagances, delusions, eventually their discovery of the strength and limitations of their emotions—and they strike a humane balance between witty gaiety and emotional intensity, a balance between a clear recognition of the frailty of human beings and an awareness of their positive qualities" (79). For Warren, Orsino's language is satirically extravagant, but also full of immediacy and vigor, while Olivia displays an emotional intensity that balances the conventions with which she is courted and the absurdity of her original intention to mourn her brother excessively.

270. **Williams, Porter, Jr..** "Mistakes in *Twelfth Night* and Their Resolution: A Study in Some Relationships of Plot and Theme." *PMLA* 76 (1961): 193–99. Selections repr. in King (no. 287) and Palmer (no. 288).

Williams argues that the mistakes of *Twelfth Night* are a subtle means of revealing underlying themes and motives: Olivia finds her way out of grieving to marriage with Sebastian through the mistake of loving Cesario, and Cesario is also the catalyst for Orsino's opening himself to real love. According to Williams, the mistakes of the limited characters block them, but the generous survive and prosper by their foolish errors.

F. Stage History and Performance Criticism.

271. Berry, Ralph. "The Season of *Twelfth Night*." In *Changing Styles in Shakespeare*, 109–19. London: Allen and Unwin, 1981.

Berry describes two models of *Twelfth Night* productions in the last century, with the change brought about by John Barton's Royal Shakespeare Company production in 1969. The first model that flourished from the nineteenth century until the seventies stressed a direct appeal to laughter and revelry. It cut all lines that create sympathy for Malvolio, as well as his final threat of vengeance and Feste's concluding song. In contrast, Berry observes, Barton's production stressed that Twelfth Night is the end of Christmas revels. In this version, Sir Toby is Maria's last chance, and Sir Toby and Sir Andrew part forever at the end. Orsino and Olivia are narcissists; Feste is a radical, and Malvolio blends "high comedy and deep emotional pain" (116). Barton's version seems to Berry an overcompensation, but Chekhov remains a dominant influence: "Through him, one catches at the implications of 'autumnal.' The subtext of autumn is winter: and one wonders if winter is not after all the right season for a setting of *Twelfth Night*" (117). For further comments on the change of interpretation, see Dawson (no. 67) and Wells (no. 281).

272. Billington, Michael, ed. *RSC Directors' Shakespeare—Approaches to "Twelfth Night" by Bill Alexander, John Barton, John Caird, Terry Hands.* London: Nick Hern Books, 1990.

After a detailed stage history of *Twelfth Night*, Billington presents an account of a two-day conversation with four Royal Shakespeare Company directors. Billington observes, "*Twelfth Night* is now and always has been an extremely elusive play. It rarely fails to afford pleasure ... But, equally, it is difficult to achieve ... its ambivalent darkness and resonant comedy" (xxx). The topics of the conversation range from the kind of play this is and "what is Illyria," to comments on all the characters, major and minor, the verse, the comedy of the yellow stockings, and what kind of research a director does to prepare for a production.

273. Granville-Barker, Harley. "Preface to *Twelfth Night*." In *More Prefaces to Shakespeare*, ed. E. M. Moore, 26–32. Princeton: Princeton Univ. Press, 1974.

Writing in 1912, Barker confesses that he likes *As You Like It* and *Much Ado* "as little as any plays he [Shakespeare] ever wrote" (26). But, for Barker, *Twelfth Night* has a happy ease in the writing, combining elements of the earlier comedies. Barker advocates a bare stage and no break in the action. He is convinced that Shakespeare let the subplot overwhelm the romantic plot, especially the part of Orsino, for whom the denouement is "all muddled up" (28). Viola *must* be played to make the audience believe she is a man, says Barker. For Barker, Toby is not a bestial sot, nor Andrew an idiot, Feste is an aging, self-acknowledged failure, and Antonio is a passionate fellow. Barker says, "The keynotes of the poetry of the play are that it is passionate and it is exquisite" (31). Finally, Barker believes all Elizabethan dramatic verse must be spoken swiftly. Many of these ideas have been highly influential.

274. Greif, Karen. "A Star Is Born: Feste on the Modern Stage." *Shakespeare Quarterly* 39 (1988): 61–78.

Using stage history, Greif traces Feste's progress from eighteenth-century productions, where his role was severely cut, to the centrality he enjoys in productions today. According to Greif, the turning point from neglect to prominence was the production of Harley Granville-Barker in 1912, where Feste starred as "the spokesman for the comedy's bittersweet undertones" (63). In Tyrone Guthrie's production of 1933, Greif says, Feste became a bitter commentator on human folly. In Guthrie's 1957 revival there was more farce in the action, Greif notes, but Feste was a grizzled figure of sadness. According to Greif, Peter Hall's staging of 1960 featured a cynical fool. Stratford, Ontario, Festes have gradually mellowed, Greif says, losing their bitter edge as they passed from the sixties to the eighties. American Festes, Greif finds, tend to be more playful, but the Royal Shakespeare Theatre has continued the fool as the central figure in *Twelfth Night*, wryly compassionate, but sounding a melancholy note, a blend of irony and sympathy. For further comments on Feste, see Wilcher (no. 65), Codden (no. 248), and Summers (no. 268).

275. Howard, Jean. "The Orchestration of *Twelfth Night*: The Rhythm of Restraint and Release." In *Shakespeare's Art of Orchestration*, 172–206. Urbana: Univ. of Illinois Press, 1984.

Howard argues that, despite having little action, the play has a high degree of complexity in its fragmentation of interest: "The progressive experience of the work has a meaningful dynamic of its own that underlies the rich thematic unity of the work" (176). She sees four movements in the play. The first introduces and contrasts Orsino, Viola, and Toby, whose dominant attitudes will be played off against one another. Howard's second movement takes the audience from Viola's first appearance at Orsino's court to Malvolio's reading of Maria's letter, a progression which creates tension as disguise and tricks confront the self-indulgence in Orsino, Malvolio, and Olivia. Howard's third movement contains most of the action and visual humor: the tricking of Malvolio, the duel, Sebastian's arrival—all gradually increase confusion and violence. In the final movement, disclosure of identity and release from egocentricity form a tenuous closure to the action that Howard contends has been a dialectic between restraint and release.

276. Osborne, Laurie E. "Antonio's Pardon." *Shakespeare Quarterly* 45 (1994): 108-14.

Osborne addresses the current debate over Antonio's relationship to Sebastian and Antonio's fate as Orsino's prisoner at the end of *Twelfth Night*. Acknowledging two present-day readings—Adelman's image of Antonio's loss of Sebastian (no. 42) and Pequigney's vision of reconciliation (no. 265)—Osborne shows that performance editions in the late eighteenth and early nineteenth centuries reveal the addition of lines in which Orsino pardons Antonio. She observes that some performances also include gestures of reunion with Sebastian. Although the problem of Antonio is consistently solved through his pardon, "Antonio's position at the end of the comedy is variable in the performance editions" (111). Often, Osborne says, Antonio is not given a place in the dance or final tableau of the actors. She concludes, "Nineteenth-century performance editions and twentieth-century critics alike pardon Antonio or try to explain him, not because Shakespeare's text requires it but because our own perceptions of homosexuality continue to evolve" (114). For the contrasting readings, see Adelman (no. 42), Traub (no. 62), and Pequigney (no. 265).

277. Osborne, Laurie E. *The Trick of Singularity: "Twelfth Night" and the Performance Editions.* Iowa City: Univ. of Iowa Press, 1996.

Osborne studies the performance editions of *Twelfth Night*, that is, published texts that present the play as performed. Many of these are very different from the Folio text. Because eighteenth- and nineteenth-century scholars assumed that *Twelfth Night* was Shakespeare's last play, dated 1614, and modern readers assume the 1601 date, Osborne concludes, "the shift in *Twelfth Night*'s date implicitly challenges any absolute assumptions about the comedy's position in the Shakespearean canon" (12). Osborne compares the text of the First Folio to a series of texts: *Bell's Shakespeare* of 1774, *A Select British Theatre* of 1815, *Inchbald's British Theatre* of 1808, *Oxberry's New English Drama* of 1821, *Cumberland's British Theatre* of 1830, and *Lacy's Acting Plays* of 1855. She shows how the texts rearrange scenes, omit some, alter character effects in accordance with changing ideas about fools, or ideal women, or homoeroticism. Osborne also explores multiple films of *Twelfth Night*, showing how seven video editions represent and manipulate the play in ways that resemble the nineteenth-century editing. She concludes with a Lacanian reading of Maria's famous letters, M. O. A. I.

278. Potter, Lois. *"Twelfth Night": Text and Performance.* London: Macmillan, 1985.

These texts consist of a critical introduction and a review of a selection of well-regarded productions that provide insight into the play. In the first part, Potter considers the factors that make *Twelfth Night* a very complex work. The rapidity and confusion of the action, the varied time schemes, the holiday unruliness, and the sense of the end of holiday as well—all contribute to a complex effect; patterns of speech and action (nonsense and fooling) reinforce this sense, Potter argues. In Part Two she tries to demonstrate her thesis that the play's theatre history is "more illuminating than its criticism" (14) by examining in detail four productions. They are John Barton's RSC production of 1969–71, Peter Gill's RSC production of 1974–75, Robin Midgley's production at the Haymarket Theatre in 1979, and the Berkeley Shakespeare Festival production by Julian Lopez-Morillas in 1981–82. The illustrated discussion concentrates on three topics: setting and costumes; romance, concluding that productions have become increasingly erotic and Viola increasingly down-to-earth; and comedy, concluding that the aging of Olivia's household has a sobering effect on the farcical aspect of *Twelfth Night*.

279. Shurgot, Michael W. *Stages of Play: Shakespeare's Theatrical Energies in Elizabethan Performance.* Newark: Univ. of Delaware Press, 1998.

Shurgot reads the plays as dynamic scripts, written for performance on the Elizabethan stage, and stresses the structural relations among scenes. In dealing with *Twelfth Night* he emphasizes the relationship between the saturnalian energy of the Malvolio action, which takes place on the *platea*, and the romantic conventions of the Orsino-Olivia action, which largely takes place on the upstage *locus*. Shurgot does not see that *Twelfth Night* resolves its conflicts. The intensity of Olivia's passion ill accords, he says, with her swift acceptance of Sebastian. He believes Orsino's rage at Viola is not resolved by her conventional submissiveness. And Shakespeare surrounds the emotional cruxes with the bloodied figures of Sir Toby and Sir Andrew, not to mention the much alienated Malvolio, thereby vitiating, for Shurgot, any reconciliation. In this reading, the end of *Twelfth Night* is artificial and schematized. "The play's convulsive Saturnalian energy becomes the paradigm of the larger structure itself, whose rapid disintegration in Act Five disables the unified joy the lovers seek and spectators expect at the end" (172). For another reading of the play's end, see Barton (no. 44); for the structure see Howard (no. 275).

280. Sinden, Donald. "Malvolio in *Twelfth Night*." In *Players of Shakespeare: Essays in Shakespearean Performance by Twelve Players with the Royal Shakespeare Company*, ed. Philip Brockbank, 41–66. Cambridge: Cambridge Univ. Press, 1985.

Sinden analyzes his performance in John Barton's production of *Twelfth Night* in 1969. He describes getting into Malvolio's skin so that Sinden's whole body reacts to Malvolio's tensions. He also provides a detailed description of how he played each scene in which he appeared. Sinden plays a tragic Malvolio for laughs.

281. Wells, Stanley. "John Barton's *Twelfth Night*, 1969–72." In *Royal Shakespeare*, 43–63. Manchester: Manchester Univ. Press, 1977.

Wells gives a very detailed positive review of John Barton's now famous production, which was distinctive at the time in its emphasis on the sadness inherent in *Twelfth Night*. Wells accents the beauty of the production, Sinden's comic brilliance as Malvolio, and Dench's poetic Viola. "Shot through with sadness though the production was, its ultimate effect was a happy one," Wells concludes (62). For other comments on this production, see Greenwald (no. 69), Berry (no. 271), and Billington (no. 272).

282. Wikander, Matthew H. "As Secret as Maidenhead: The Boy-Actress in *Twelfth Night*." *Comparative Drama* 20 (1986): 349–63.

Wikander argues that the apprentice boy-actress, who is a real adolescent in a highly ambiguous state (with his voice about to change), embodies Viola's dramatic predicament: "The searching and uncertainty of Viola are those of the boy-actress at the height of his career" (354). Viola demonstrates the dangers of acting, Wikander says. Yet, Wikander points out, several roles are open to the adult actor, depending on how his career develops: Olivia's role as lady, Malvolio's, or Feste's. For further comments on boy actresses, see Shapiro (no. 36).

See also nos. 66–76

G. Adaptations.

283. Burnaby, Charles. *Love Betray'd; Or, the Agreable Disapointment A Comedy*. London: D. Brown, 1703. Facsimile reprint, London: Cornmarket, 1969.

Burnaby makes wholesale changes in Shakespeare's play to adapt *Twelfth Night's* complexity to eighteenth-century taste. Only fifty lines of Shakespeare are retained, and all verse is reduced to prose. For details, see Odell (no. 72).

284. Molloy, Charles. *The Half-Pay Officers.* London: A. Bettesworth, 1720. Facsimile reprint, London: Cornmarket, 1969.

This three-act farce combines characters derived from Pistol and Fluellen in a plot based on Davenant's *Love and Honour*, with lines taken from *Much Ado* and other Shakespeare texts. There is a duel that may have been suggested by that between Cesario and Sir Andrew. For brief comments, see Odell (no. 72).

H. Pedagogy.

285. Cookson, Linda, and Bryan Loughrey, eds. *Critical Essays on "Twelfth Night."* London: Longman Group, 1990.

This series offers short essays commissioned from teachers and theatre practitioners as models for high-school and college students who seek to develop skills in essay writing using the text of Shakespeare's play as the basis for topics. Each essay is followed by questions that relate the essay to the play text. The book ends with a practical guide to essay writing, suggestions for further reading, and a brief style sheet.

286. Coursen, H. R. *Teaching Shakespeare with Film and Television, A Guide.* Westport: Greenwood Press, 1997.

Coursen writes for all teachers—high school through college—who use films of any sort in teaching Shakespeare. He makes distinctions between cinematic films and television productions and provides guides to evaluation. Materials are suggested for research. In one chapter, Coursen presents different readings of the Madhouse scene in *Twelfth Night* (4.2), using four productions: John Dexter's BBC film in 1970, John Gorrie's BBC film in 1988, Kenneth Branagh's Renaissance Theatre Company production in 1988, and Trevor Nunn's of 1996.

See also nos. 76a–78, 216.

I. Collections.

287. King, Walter N., ed. *Twentieth Century Interpretations of "Twelfth Night": A Collection of Critical Essays.* Englewood Cliffs, N.J.: Prentice-Hall, 1968.

Longer interpretations include the work of C. L. Barber (no. 28), Sylvan Barnet, H. B. Charlton, H. C. Goddard (no. 49), John Hollander (no. 256), Clifford Leech, Julian Markels, Leo Salingar (no. 266), Joseph Summers (no.

268), and Porter Williams, Jr. (no. 270). Shorter excerpts are by Alan Downer, Harold Goddard (no. 49), Leslie Hotson (no. 225), G. K. Hunter (no. 257), Moelwyn Merchant, and Mark Van Doren (no. 63).

288. Palmer, D. J., ed. *Shakespeare: "Twelfth Night," A Casebook*. London: Macmillan, 1972.

The collection contains short selections from texts, commentary, adaptations, and criticism from 1602 to 1912. These include comments by John Manningham, by Leonard Digges, by Samuel Pepys, by Samuel Johnson, by William Hazlitt, by Charles Lamb, by Émile Montegut, and by Harley Granville-Barker (no. 273); a snippet from Burnaby's *Love Betray'd* (no. 283); James Boaden's comment on Mrs. Jordan as Viola (1837), Sir Edward Russell's comment on Irving as Malvolio (1884), William Winter's comment on Ada Rehan as Viola (1895), and John Masefield's comment on Granville-Barker's production (1912). Longer twentieth-century studies include work by C. L. Barber (no. 28), M. C. Bradbrook, A. C. Bradley, J. R. Brown (no. 46), H. B. Charlton, Bertrand Evans (no. 48), John Hollander (no. 256), Leslie Hotson (no. 225), D. J. Palmer (no. 234), Joseph Summers (no. 268), and Porter Williams (no. 270).

289. Wells, Stanley, ed. *"Twelfth Night": Critical Essays*. New York: Garland Publishing, 1986.

This collection presents much classic commentary on the play, including work by C. L. Barber (no. 28), Anne Barton (no. 44), Max Beerbohm, A. C. Bradley, J. R. Brown, Bertrand Evans (no. 48), Harley Granville-Barker (no. 273), Karen Greif (no. 254), Jorg Hasler, Leslie Hotson (no. 225), Harold Jenkins (no. 261), Charles Lamb, Alexander Leggatt (no. 56), Harry Levin (no. 263), Henry Morley, J. B. Priestly, Leo Salingar (no. 266), Arthur C. Sprague, Roy Walker, and Virginia Woolf.

290. White, R. S., ed. *"Twelfth Night": New Casebooks*. New York: St. Martin's Press, 1996.

This series is concerned "with modern critical theory and its effect on current approaches to the study of literature. Each New Casebook editor has been asked to select a sequence of essays which will introduce the reader to the new critical approaches to the text ... and also illuminate the rich interchange between critical theory and critical practice that characterises so much current writing about literature." (ix) White has chosen work by the following: Michael Bristol, Dympna Callaghan (no. 220), Barbara Everett (no. 250), Stephen Greenblatt (no. 253), Geoffrey Hartman (no. 242), Elliot Krieger (no. 55), Cristina Malcolmson (no. 233), and Leonard Tennenhouse. White's introduction argues that "the real drift of criticism over the last decades has been inexorably in the direction of reader response theories, and the blossoming of a plurality of individual readings" (9–10). White sees the play as postmodern in its representation of the slipperiness of language, the fickleness and arbitrariness of sexual desire, the manifest construction of meaning in Malvolio's reading of Maria's letter, the critique of romantic love, and the aristocratic society challenged by bourgeois *arrivistes* and the Puritan spirit as well.

J. Bibliography and Concordance.

291. Donno, Elizabeth Story. "*Twelfth Night.*" In *The Shakespearean International Yearbook*, ed. W. R. Elton and J. M. Mucciolo, 322–28. Aldershot: Ashgate Publishing, 1999.

This brief essay is a review of criticism of the last twenty-five years in about twenty articles, including Barton (no. 44), Berry (no. 247), Callaghan (no. 220), Greenblatt (no. 253), Greif (no. 254), Hartman (no. 242), Hutson (no. 259), Jardine (no. 260), and Malcolmson (no. 233). Donno is scornful of much recent commentary on the play because it scants *Twelfth Night*'s aesthetic and dramatic merits. She observes how all the major characters have become contested subjects, especially Malvolio, who is either a tragic figure or the object of sport. For Donno, the comedy, once thought joyous and festive, is now seen as presenting a bleak picture of the human condition. Donno questions some of the critics' use of evidence, and she concludes that most of the pieces she reviews are "tendentious because of their deriving, or imposing, ideological concepts from or onto the text" (327).

292. Howard-Hill, T. H., ed. *"Twelfth Night": A Concordance to the Text of the First Folio.* Oxford: Clarendon, 1969.

A separate volume is devoted to each of the twenty-four plays in the Oxford Shakespeare Concordances, which are based on the Oxford Old Spelling Shakespeare. "The copy for the concordance to *Twelfth Night* was the Lee facsimile of the First Folio (1902)" (xi). The volume "takes account of every word in the text, and represents their occurrence by frequency counts, line numbers, and reference lines, or a selection of these according to the interest of the particular word" (v).

See also nos. 82–86.

INDEX I: AUTHORS AND EDITORS (FOR SECTIONS II–V)

Adelman, Janet, 42
Allen, John, 176
Anderson, Linda, 246
Andreas, James, 206a
Astington, John, 219
Auden, W. H., 210

Ball, Robert, 72
Bamber, Linda, 43
Barber, C. L., 28, 149, 150, 151, 287, 288, 289
Barish, Jonas, 171
Barnet, Sylvan, 115, 151, 287
Barton, Anne, 44, 79, 289
Bate, Jonathan, 197
Beckman, Margaret, 116
Beehler, Sharon, 76a
Beerbohm, Max, 289
Belsey, Catherine, 29
Bennett, Robert, 91
Berger, Harry, 177, 211
Bergeron, David, 80
Berry, E. I., 92, 149
Berry, Ralph, 45, 117, 152, 247, 271
Bethell, S. L., 150
Billington, Michael, 272
Billington, Sandra, 30
Bloom, Harold, 149
Boaden, James, 288
Boas, Frederick, 151
Booth, Stephen, 76a, 240
Bowe, John, 127

Bradbrook, M. C., 81, 288
Bradby, G. F., 151
Bradley, A. C., 288, 289
Branagh, Kenneth, 191
Brandes, Georg, 151, 152
Braunmuller, A. R., 119
Brereton, Austin, 152
Brissenden, Alan, 87
Bristol, Michael, 290
Brockbank, Philip, 127, 152, 213, 280
Brode, Douglas, 66
Brooke, S. A., 151
Brooks, Harold, 81
Brown, John R., 31, 39, 46, 79, 150, 151, 288, 289
Buhler, Stephen, 76b
Bulman, J. C., 119, 128, 152, 194, 200
Burnaby, Charles, 283, 288
Burnett, Mark, 136
Bush, Geoffrey, 151

Callaghan, Dympna, 58, 61, 220, 290
Campbell, O. J., 151
Capell, Edward, 152
Carroll, Lewis, 157
Carroll, William C., 80, 118, 149, 221
Cerasano, S. P., 172, 211
Chambers, E. K., 151
Chambers, R. W., 81
Champion, Larry, 47, 82
Charlton, H. B., 150, 287, 288
Charney, Maurice, 80, 221, 230, 236

INDEX I: AUTHORS AND EDITORS

Child, Harold, 158
Cirillo, Albert, 93, 151
Clapp, Henry, 151
Clark, Cumberland, 152
Clarke, M. C., 151
Clubb, Louise G., 80
Codden, Karin, 248
Cohen, Ralph A., 76a, 76b
Cohen, Robert, 76c
Coleridge, Samuel Taylor, 151
Collier, J. P., 152
Collins, Howard, 203
Collins, Michael J., 76b, 76d
Cook, Carol, 178
Cookson, Linda, 207, 285
Cordner, Michael, 181
Coursen, H. R., 128, 194, 195, 200, 286
Cox, John, 155, 192
Craik, T. W., 215
Crane, Mary T., 111
Crane, Milton, 151
Crewe, Jonathan, 249
Crick, John, 210
Croall, Jonathan, 193
Crowl, Samuel, 129

Daniel, George, 151
Davenant, William, 204
Davis, James, 76d, 206a, 209
Davis, Walter, 149, 210
Dawson, Anthony, 67, 152, 179
Dennis, Carl, 180
Derrick, Patty, 130
Dessen, Alan, 131, 152
Digges, Leonard, 288
Dobree, Bonamy, 81
Donno, Elizabeth, 213, 291
Dowden, Edward, 151
Downer, Alan, 287
Drakakis, John, 29
Draper, John, 151, 222
Dusinberre, Juliet, 94, 160

Eagleton, Terence, 241
Elam, Keir, 40, 223
Erickson, Peter, 42, 95, 151
Evans, Bertrand, 48, 151, 288, 289
Evans, Faith, 138
Evans, Gareth Lloyd, 31, 79
Everett, Barbara, 181, 211, 250, 290
Ewbank, Inga-Stina, 79

Faucit, Helena, 151, 152
Fergusson, Francis, 210
Fineman, Joel, 251
Fink, Z. S., 151
Finucci, Valeria, 124
Fletcher, George, 71
Foakes, R. A., 79
Forker, Charles, 149
Freeburg, Victor, 152
Freedman, Barbara, 80, 252
Freund, Elizabeth, 80
Frye, Northrop, 32, 210
Furness, H. H., 151, 156, 214

Garber, Marjorie, 76a, 80, 119, 149
Gardner, Helen, 81, 120, 150, 151
Garrett, John, 120
Gay, Penny, 68, 211
Gentleman, Francis, 151, 152
Gervinus, G. G., 151, 152
Gibson, Rex, 76e
Gielgud, John, 196
Gilbert, Allan, 182
Gildon, Charles, 151, 152
Goddard, Harold, 49, 149, 151, 210, 287
Goldsmith, Robert, 121
Gordon, George, 152
Gough, Melinda, 161
Grant, Cathy, 76e
Granville-Barker, Harley, 273, 288, 289
Gras, Henk, 224
Greenblatt, Stephen, 253, 290
Greenwald, Michael, 69

Greg, W. W., 151
Greif, Karen, 254, 274, 289
Griffith, Elisabeth, 151
Grindon, R. E., 152

Halio, Jay, 122, 150, 151, 153
Hamer, Mary, 132
Hapgood, Robert, 208
Harris, Bernard, 31, 44, 79
Hartman, Geoffrey, 242, 290
Hartwig, Joan, 255
Hasler, Jorg, 289
Hassel, R. Chris, 149
Hattaway, Michael, 88, 197
Hawkes, Terence, 80
Hawkins, Harriet, 80
Hawkins, Sherman, 50
Hayles, Nancy, 51, 151
Hazlitt, William, 151, 288
Henley, W. E., 152
Herford, Charles, 152
Hieatt, Charles, 96
Hockey, Dorothy, 183, 210
Hodges, Devon, 149
Hoenselaars, A. J., 160, 169
Hogan, Charles, 70
Holding, Edith, 145
Holland, Peter, 181
Hollander, John, 256, 287, 288
Horowitz, David, 210
Hotson, Leslie, 225, 287, 288, 289
Howard, Jean, 97, 162, 211, 275
Howard-Hill, T. H., 154, 212, 292
Hudson, H. N., 151
Hunt, John D., 79
Hunt, Leigh, 74
Hunt, Maurice, 226, 227
Hunter, G. K., 151, 257, 287
Hunter, R. G., 210
Hurd, Richard, 151
Hurworth, Angela, 228
Huston, J. Dennis, 184, 258
Hutson, Lorna, 259

Ingram, Raymond, 76e

Jackson, Russell, 71, 202
Jameson, Anna, 151
Jamieson, Michael, 133, 152
Jardine, Lisa, 260
Jenkins, Harold, 81, 123, 150, 151, 185, 261, 289
Jensen, Ejner, 52
Johnson, Charles, 146, 152
Johnson, Samuel, 152, 288
Jorgensen, Paul, 173

Kahn, Coppélia, 42, 251
Kemp, Peter, 200
Kennedy, Dennis, 134
Kerrigan, John, 181, 262
Kerrigan, William, 124
Kimbrough, Robert, 53, 151
King, Walter, 186, 210, 287
Kiniry, Malcolm, 80
Knight, G. W., 81
Knowles, Richard, 89, 98
Ko, Yu Jin, 229
Kolbe, F. C., 152
Kolin, Philip, 83
Kott, Jan, 54, 99, 151
Kreider, P. V., 151
Krieger, Elliott, 55, 151, 187, 290
Kronenfeld, Judy, 100

Lamb, Charles, 74, 288, 289
Lamb, Mary Ellen, 80, 230, 231
Latham, Agnes, 90
Latham, Grace, 152
Lea, Kathleen, 33
Leach, Susan, 77
Leech, Clifford, 81, 287
Leggatt, Alexander, 56, 151, 289
Lehmann, Courtney, 198
Lennox, Patricia, 135
Levenson, Jill, 197
Levin, Harry, 263, 289

INDEX I: AUTHORS AND EDITORS

Lewalski, Barbara, 163, 232
Lewis, Cynthia, 243
Lifson, Martha, 112; *see also* Ronk, Martha, 113
Lothian, J. N., 215
Loughrey, Bryan, 207, 285

MacCary, Thomas, 57
McCloskey, Susan, 200
McCollum, W. G., 174, 210
McDonald, Russ, 76b, 114
McEachern, Claire, 164
McFarland, Thomas, 101
McMurtry, Jo, 78
McPeek, James, 210
Maginn, William, 151
Mahood, M. M., 84
Malcolmson, Cristina, 233, 290
Manningham, John, 288
Mares, F. H., 157
Markels, Julian, 287
Marrapodi, Michele, 160, 169
Marriette, Amelia, 136
Marshall, Cynthia, 125
Masefield, John, 152, 288
Mason, Pamela, 199
Mattern, Evelyn J., 89
Matthews, Brander, 152
Maurer, Margaret, 147, 152
Mehl, Dieter, 197
Mellamphy, Ninian, 80
Merchant, Moelwyn, 287
Millard, Barbara, 153
Miller, James, 205
Mincoff, Marco, 102, 150
Moglen, Helene, 264
Molloy, Charles, 284
Montegut, Émile, 288
Montrose, Louis, 103, 151
Moore, E. M., 273
Morley, Henry, 289
Muir, Kenneth, 81, 151
Murry, J. Middleton, 81

Myhill, Nova, 165

Neely, Carol, 58, 188
Nevo, Ruth, 34, 80
Noble, Richmond, 152
Novy, Marianne, 59, 135
Nugent, S. Georgia, 80
Nutall, A. D., 79

O'Brien, Peggy, 76b
O'Connor, Marion F., 162
Odell, George, 72
Olive, David, 76e
Orgel, Stephen, 35
Osborne, Laurie, 166, 276, 277
Oz, Avraham, 80

Paglia, Camille, 149
Palmer, D. J., 79, 104, 151, 234, 288
Palmer, John, 210
Parker, Patricia, 242
Pepys, Samuel, 288
Pequigney, Joseph, 265
Peterson, Douglas, 80
Phileas, Peter, 151
Potter, Lois, 278
Powell, Jocelyn, 79
Priestly, J. B., 152, 289
Prouty, Charles, 167

Quiller-Couch, Arthur, 151, 158

Rackin, Phyllis, 60
Richards, David, 200
Richardson, William, 151
Richmond, Hugh M., 151, 168
Rickman, Alan, 137
Riemer, A. P., 151
Riggio, Milla, 76b, 208
Roberts, Jeanne A., 80, 152
Rocklin, Edward, 76a
Ronk, Martha, 113; *see also* Lifson, Martha, 112

Rossiter, A. P., 81, 189, 210
Rothwell, Kenneth, 73
Rozett, Martha T., 76b
Russell, Edward, 71, 288
Rutter, Carol, 138

Sajdak, Bruce, 85
Salgādo, Gāmini, 74
Salomone, Ronald, 76d, 206a, 209
Salingar, Leo, 80, 169, 266, 287, 289
Sauer, David, 76b
Schafer, Elizabeth, 201
Schanzer, Ernest, 81
Scheil, Katherine, 148, 206
Schlegel, A. W., 151
Schwartz, Murray, 251
Schwartz, Regina, 124
Scott, Mark, 151
Scoufos, Alice-Lyle, 105, 151
Scragg, Leah, 235
Sen Gupta, S. C., 151
Shapiro, Michael, 36
Shaw, Catherine, 80
Shaw, Fiona, 139
Shaw, George Bernard, 74, 151, 152
Shurgot, Michael, 279
Siegel, Paul, 80, 236
Sinden, Donald, 280
Skrebels, Paul, 209
Slights, Camille, 267
Smallwood, Robert, 86, 137, 139, 141, 142, 202
Smith, Bruce, 216
Smith, James, 190, 210
Smith, Peter, 237
Snider, D. J., 151, 152
Snyder, Susan, 80
Soule, Lesley, 106
Speight, Robert, 75
Sprague, A. C., 289
Spurgeon, Caroline, 175
Staebler, Warren, 151
Stamm, Rudolph, 140

Steed, Maggie, 202
Stevenson, Juliet, 139
Stoll, E. E., 151
Storey, Graham, 210
Summers, Joseph, 268, 287, 288
Suzuki, Mihoko, 61
Swinden, Patrick, 126, 151
Sypher, Wylie, 210

Taylor, A. B., 238
Tennant, David, 141
Tennenhouse, Leonard, 290
Terry, Ellen, 152
Thompson, Marvin, 144
Thompson, Ruth, 144
Thompson, Sophie, 142
Thomson, Virgil, 210
Tomarken, Edward, 133, 147, 152
Traci, Philip, 107
Traub, Valerie, 62
Traugott, John, 170
Traversi, Derek, 81
Trousdale, Marion, 80
Turner, Robert K., 218

Ulrici, Herman, 151, 152
Ungerer, Gustav, 244

Van Doren, Mark, 63, 151, 287
Vickers, Brian, 41

Walker, James, 217
Walker, Roy, 289
Ward, John P., 143
Warren, Roger, 217, 269
Wayne, Valerie, 233

Wells, Stanley, 79, 217, 281, 289
Welsford, Enid, 37, 151
Westlund, Joseph, 64
Weston, Murray, 76e
Wey, James, 210
Wheeler, Richard, 239

White, R. S., 290
Whiter, Walter, 151, 152
Wickham, Glynne, 144, 152
Wikander, Matthew, 282
Wilcher, Robert, 65, 151
Wilde, Oscar, 74
Williams, Porter, Jr., 270, 287, 288
Williamson, Marilyn, 38, 108
Willis, Susan, 152
Wilson, E. M., 190
Wilson, John Dover, 151, 158
Wilson, Richard, 109

Wingate, Charles, 152

Winter, William, 76, 288
Wofford, Susanne, 114
Woolf, Virginia, 289
Wray, Ramona, 136
Wynne-Davies, Marion, 172, 211

Yearling, Elizabeth, 245
Young, David, 110, 151

Zimmerman, Susan, 260
Zitner, Sheldon, 159

INDEX II: SUBJECTS

The following indexes the contents of the annotations, nos. 28–292, in Sections II–V; references to characters are to extended comments.

Alexander, Bill, 68, 199, 272
anagorisis, 34
Anderson, Mary, 130
androgyny, 53, 60, 95, 99, 106, 118, 249
Anglin, Margaret, 76
Annunciation, 227
antitheatricality, 60, 162, 165
Antonio, 42, 55, 62, 265, 276
Antoon, A. J., 194
"Apolonius and Silla," *see* Riche, Barnabe
Arcadia, 54, 134
Arden, Forest of, 55, 117, 120, 122, 123, 128, 129, 134, 135, 136
Arden of Faversham, 61
Ariosto, Lodovico, *Orlando Furioso*, 156, 159, 160, 161, 166, 223

aristocracy, 49, 55, 100, 103, 109, 187, 231, 233, 248, 268

Armin, Robert, 31, 111
art and nature, 104, 113, 128
As You Like It (act and scene)
—(1.2), 39, 127
—(2.3), 100
—(2.4), 54, 64, 104, 110
—(2.5), 91, 120, 125, 137
—(2.7), 104, 109
—(3.2), 40, 55, 65, 100, 113
—(3.4), 139, 142
—(4.1), 39, 62, 114
—(4.3), 51, 98, 105, 139, 142
—(5.1), 111
—(5.2), 119
—(5.4), 39, 44, 51, 56, 103, 108, 112

Ashcroft, Peggy, 68, 133
Athenaeum, The, 152
Audrey, 65, 100, 135, 144

Bandello, Matteo, 156, 157, 159, 166, 169, 214
Barber, C. L., 52; see also author index
Barton, Anne, 291; see also author index
Barton, John, 44, 68, 69, 199, 271, 272, 278, 281
Bates College performance of *As You Like It*, 195
bawdry, 87, 196, 220, 235, 244
BBC films, 199, 200, 286
Beatrice, 71, 166, 167, 170, 171, 172, 181, 186, 192, 202
Belle-Forest, Francois de, 156
Bell's Shakespeare, 277
Bembo, Pietro, Cardinal, 163
Benedick, 166, 167, 170, 171, 181, 186, 190, 192, 193
Benson, Frank, 72
Bergner, Elizabeth, 66, 73
Berkeley (Calif.) Shakespeare Festival, 278
Berry, Ralph, 291; see also author index
Betterton, Thomas, 72
Beverley, Peter, *Ariodanto and Ieneura*, 167
Bevington, David, 216
Bibbiena, Bernardo Dovizi da, 223
Black Act of 1723, 148
boy actresses, 35, 36, 60, 97, 282
Branagh, Kenneth, 66, 73, 195, 197, 198, 286; see also author index
Burge, Stuart, 200

Caird, John, 68, 142, 272
Callaghan, Dympna, 291; see also author index
Campbell, Lady Archibald, 133
carnival, 109
Castiglione, Baldassare, *The Courtier*, 157, 159, 163, 223

Celia, 135, 139, 142
Cesario, 227, 233, 253, 260, 262, 282; see also Viola
Chapman, George, *Bussy D'Ambois*, 91; *Gentleman Usher*, 259
Cheek-by-Jowl Company, 133
Chekhov, Anton, 271
Christmas season, 222, 232
Cibber, Colley, 72
class (social status), 55, 61, 100, 109, 111, 231, 233, 259, 260
Claudio, 161, 166, 167, 170, 172, 174, 178, 179, 180, 181, 186, 190, 199
Clifford, Anne, Lady, 231
clown, 54, 111, 241; see also fool
comedy, closed world in, 50; *commedia dell'arte*, 33; Donatan structure, 34; festive, 28; form of, 44, 45; green world in, 32; new comedic structure, 32; romantic, 56; Terentian, 259
cony-catching, 228; see also cutpurse
Copeau, Jacques, 75, 133
Corin, 65, 96, 100, 108, 123
Courtier, The, see Castiglione, Baldassare
critical approaches
—anthropological, 28, 262, 263, 267
—feminist, 29, 38, 51, 53, 58, 59, 60, 95, 106, 164, 178, 188, 220
—generic, 34, 43, 44, 47, 50, 93, 96, 101, 108, 110, 161, 166, 170
—Marxist, 55, 100, 109, 187, 198
—materialist, 35, 36, 51, 61, 97, 162, 233, 235, 248, 260
—mythic, 32, 98, 104, 118, 221, 230, 234, 238
—new critical, 56, 63, 92, 116, 122, 123, 171, 173, 185, 256, 257, 266, 268
—new historicist, 103, 111, 172, 228, 231, 253, 262
—post-modern, 240, 241, 242, 249, 250, 290
—psychoanalytic, 42, 57, 62, 64, 112, 114, 124, 125, 178, 239, 249, 251, 252,

258, 264, 265, 277; Freudian, 178, 264; Kleinian, 64; Lacanian, 125, 252, 277
—religious, 105, 163, 219, 226, 227, 229, 232, 255
—rhetorical, 40, 112, 113, 114, 174, 179, 243, 244, 245
—thematic, 45, 49, 63, 123, 180, 183, 189, 190, 250, 270
crossdressing, 35, 36, 51, 53, 60, 97, 249, 282
cuckoldry, 38, 103, 178, 251
Cumberland's British Theatre, 277
Cushman, Charlotte, 133
cutpurse, 235; see also cony-catching
Czinner, Paul, 66, 73

Davenant, William, 72, 155, 203, 206; see also author index
Dench, Judi, 69, 199, 201, 281
Dexter, John, 133, 286
disguise, 35, 51, 53, 264
Dogberry, 176, 190, 195, 206a
Don John, 161, 162, 178, 184, 205
Don Pedro, 161, 162, 171, 174, 178, 184, 190, 198
doubles, 125, 136, 228, 251; see also twins

Echo, 234, 238
Edwards, Gale, 201
Edzard, Christine, 66, 73, 135, 136, 195
Elizabeth I, 94, 225, 244
Elliott, Michel, 68
Epiphany, Feast of, 232
eunuchs, 219, 223
Evans, Edith, 132, 133
Eyre, Ronald, 68

Fairie Queene, The, see Spenser, Edmund
Faucit, Helena, 71, 133
Feste, 31, 65, 231, 241, 248, 255, 268, 274

festivals, 28, 30, 219
festivity, 248
Fletcher, George, 71
fool, 30, 31, 37, 65, 111, 121, 241, 248, 274, 277; see also clown, Touchstone, Feste
Forde, Emanuel, *Famous History of Parismus*, 217
Foucault, Michel, 198
Francis I, 168
fratricide, 124, 251
Freud, see critical approaches, psychoanalytic
Fried, Yakov, 73
Frye, Northrop, 50, 52; see also author index

Gamelyn, 89
Ganymede, 51, 106, 118, 119, 128
Garrick, David, 72, 156
gender, 29, 35, 36, 43, 51, 58, 77, 83, 97, 99, 124, 162, 178, 220, 233, 260
Gentleman's Magazine, The, 152
Gielgud, John, 68, 75, 192, 193, 196, 199
Gill, Peter, 68, 278
Goodbody, Buzz, 68
Gordon, George, 152
Gorrie, John, 286
Gramsci, Antonio, 198
Greenblatt, Stephen, 291
Greene, Robert, 89
Greif, Karen, 291
Guazzo, Stephano, 223
Guthrie, Tyrone, 274

Half-Pay Officers, The, 284
Hall, Peter, 68, 75, 274
Hand, Terry, 68, 199, 272
Harington, John, 94, 156, 159, 160
Hartman, Geoffrey, 291
Haymarket Theatre, 278
Heilbrun, Carolyn, 53

Hepburn, Katharine, 133
Heptameron of Marguerite de Navarre, 168
Hercules, 98
Hero, 77, 161, 163, 166, 172, 177, 178, 181
homoeroticism, homosexuality, 36, 62, 107, 114, 264, 265, 276, 277
Hooker, Richard, 226
Hutson, Lorna, 291
Hymen, masque of, 67, 108, 112, 118, 125, 128,

Illyria, 44, 217, 232, 234, 272
Inchbald's British Theatre, 277
Ingannati, Gl', 214, 217
Irving, Henry, 72, 74, 76, 156, 288

Jacobi, Derek, 68
Jacques, 46, 67, 91, 96, 120, 121, 125, 128, 137
Jameson, Frederick, 198
Jardine, Lisa, 291
John, Don, of Austria (natural brother of Philip II of Spain), 168
Johnson, Charles, 72, 145, 147, 148; see also author index
Jones, David, 68
Jonson, Ben, *Epicoene*, 60; *Every Man Out of his Humour*, 224, 256
Jordan, Dorothy, 74, 76, 133, 156, 288

Kaut-Howson, Helena, 201
Kean, Charles, 72
Kemble, John Philip, 72, 74
Kemp, Peter, 200
Kemp, Will, 31, 111
"Kill Claudio," *Much Ado* 4.1, 170, 171, 192, 202, 208
Knight, Charles, 71

Lacan, see critical approaches, psychoanalytic

Lacy's Acting Plays, 277
Langham, Michael, 68
Langtry, Lillie, 72
Law Against Lovers, The, 72, 203, 204, 206; see also Davenant, William
Leigh, Vivien, 68, 75
Leonato, 164, 169, 171, 174, 190, 205
Levi-Strauss, Claude, 267
Lindsay, Robert, 200
Lodge, Thomas, *Rosalynde*, 87, 88, 89, 90, 92, 102, 115
London Gazette, 152
Lopez-Morillas, Julian, 278
Love Betray'd, 72, 283, 288
Love in a Forest, 72, 145, 146, 147, 148, 152; see also Johnson, Charles
Love's Labour's Won, 144
Love's Metamorphosis, 221
Lunghi, Cherie, 200
Lyly, John, 60, 89, 90; *Gallathea*, 60, 221

Macready, William, 72, 74, 133
malcontent, 91
male bonding, 42, 103, 114, 178, 265, 276
Malvolio, 40, 48, 226, 257, 280; gulling of (*Twelfth Night* 3.4), 219, 220, 228, 233, 235, 236, 243, 244, 246, 247, 254, 255, 263
Manchester Royal Exchange, 201
Margaret, 158, 182, 184
Marguerite de Navarre, Princess, 168; see *Heptameron*
Maria, 228, 232, 233, 246, 247, 254, 263, 271
Marlowe, Julia, 71, 72, 76, 130
Marston, John, *The Malcontent*, 91
Maydes Metamorphosis, The, 221
melancholy, 91, 116, 125, 128, 232, 239, 251, 252, 274
Meres, Francis, *Palladis Tamia*, 89, 144, 156, 159

INDEX II: SUBJECTS

Messina, 177, 181, 186, 190, 210
metamorphosis, 60, 118, 221, 230
Midgely, Robin, 278
Miller, James, *The Universal Passion*, 72, 156; *see also* author index
misrule, 37, 266
M. O. A. I., 237, 240, 277
Modjeska, Helen, 130
mourning, melancholia, *see* melancholy
Mozart, W. A., 269
Much Ado about Nothing (act and scene)
—(1.1), 171, 198, 202
—(1.3), 168
—(2.1), 174
—(2.2), 161, 184
—(2.3), 162, 184, 185
—(3.1), 162, 177, 185
—(3.2), 185
—(3.3), 169, 176, 185, 190
—(4.1), 163, 164, 170, 171, 172, 178, 182, 186, 187, 192, 202
—(4.2), 190
—(5.1), 174
—(5.2), 181
—(5.4), 166, 180
music, 87, 88, 89, 90, 152, 157, 215, 216, 217, 256
"Music and Shakespeare," 152
mutuality, 59, 267

narcissism, 50, 64, 228, 234, 264
Narcissus, myth of, 230, 234, 238
Nashe, Thomas, *Summer's Last Will and Testament*, 28
National Theatre, 133, 134, 199
Navarre, Princess Marguerite de, *see Heptameron*
Neilson, Adelaide, 71, 76
Neoplatonism, 105, 163
Noble, Adrian, 68, 129, 132, 137, 138, 139
Noli me tangere, 229
nothing, 169, 173, 179, 183, 185, 189

Nunn, Trevor, 66, 73, 134, 199, 286

Oliver, 104, 105, 109, 117, 119, 124
Olivia, 36, 220, 227, 238, 244, 258, 260, 261, 262, 269, 279
Olivier, Laurence, 66, 68, 73, 75
Orlando, 98, 100, 103, 105, 109, 119, 127
Orlando Furioso, *see* Ariosto, Ludovico
Orsino, 43, 225, 234, 238, 240, 245, 256, 260, 261, 273, 279
Orsino, Virginio, Duke of Bracciano, 225
Ovid, *Metamorphoses*, 221, 230, 234, 238
Oxberry's New English Drama, 72, 277

Painter, William, *Palace of Pleasure*, 168
Papp, Joseph, 194
pastoral, 46, 63, 88, 93, 96, 100, 101, 103, 104, 108, 110, 128
patriarchy, 38, 58, 95, 97, 135, 164, 178, 220, 260
Phebe and Silvius, 51, 92, 96, 135
Phelps, Samuel, 72, 76
Pimlott, Steven, 141
Playfair, Nigel, 133
plot and subplot, *Much Ado*, 166, 167, 181, 184, 186, 188; *Twelfth Night*, 238, 254, 257, 258, 262, 266, 279
Pritchard, Hannah, 156
Providence, 226, 255
Puritans, 28, 49, 60, 216, 219, 226, 236, 243, 290

Rabelais, Francois, 94
Redgrave, Michael, 68
Redgrave, Vanessa, 68, 132, 133
Rehan, Ada, 71, 74, 76, 130, 288
Renaissance Theatre Company, 199, 201, 286
Riche, Barnabe, "Apolonius and Silla," in *Riche's Farewell to a Militarie Profession*, 214, 215, 217

Rigg, Diana, 68
Rinaldo (a hero in *Orlando Furioso*), 170
Robertson, Forbes, 74
Robin Hood, 89, 109
Rosalind, 29, 49, 71, 92, 95, 102, 106, 116, 118, 126, 130, 132, 138, 139, 142, 149
Rosalinda, 133
Royal Shakespeare Company, 127, 129, 133, 134, 137, 139, 141, 142, 199, 201, 202, 271, 272, 274, 278, 280, 281

Saturnalia, 28, 266, 278, 279
scapegoats, 50, 61, 178, 263
Schaubühne (Berlin theatre), 133, 134
Sebastian, 42, 44, 53, 54, 55, 221, 239, 249, 260, 265, 267, 270, 276
Secchi, Nicolo, *Gl'Inganni*, 214
Select British Theatre, 277
service, 231, 260, 267,
sexuality, 29, 35, 36, 51, 107, 249, 251, 253, 264, 265
Shakespeare, Hamnet, 239
Shakespeare, William
—*All's Well That Ends Well*, 47, 64, 215
—*Comedy of Errors*, 47, 50, 56, 184
—*Hamlet*, 49, 149, 251
—1 & 2 *Henry IV*, 28, 149
—*Henry V*, 284
—*King Lear*, 110, 120, 129, 164, 173
—*Love's Labor's Lost*, 28, 50, 56, 144, 152, 184
—*Measure for Measure*, 47, 64, 68, 204, 206
—*The Merchant of Venice*, 28, 38, 50, 56, 64, 86, 239, 265
—*The Merry Wives of Windsor*, 86
—*A Midsummer Night's Dream*, 28, 47, 50, 56, 146, 184
—*Othello*, 45, 179

—*The Taming of the Shrew*, 56, 68, 184
—*The Tempest*, 47, 110
—*The Two Gentlemen of Verona*, 47, 50, 63
—*The Winter's Tale*, 47, 57, 110, 215
Shaw, Glen Byam, 68, 133
Siddons, Sarah, 76
Sidney, Philip, 89, 170, 214
Silvius, *see* Phebe and
Sinden, Donald, 281; *see also* author index
slander, 172
Smith, Maggie, 133
social status, *see* class
Sothern, Edward, 72, 76
Spectator, The, 152
Spenser, Edmund, *The Fairie Queene*, 156, 157, 159, 161, 170
Stein, Peter, 133, 134
Stevenson, Juliet, 132, 138; *see also* author index
Stone, Oliver, *Wall Street*, 136
Stratford, Ontario, Shakespeare Festival, 131, 133, 195, 274
Suffolk, Duchess of, 259
Supervielle, Jules, 133
Sutton, Shaun, 200
Suzman, Janet, 68

Terentian comedy, *see* comedy
Terry, Ellen, 71, 72, 74, 76; *see also* author index
Theophrastus, 224
Thompson, Sophie, 142
Times, The (London), 152
Toby, 222, 232, 236, 240, 245, 246, 254, 255, 262, 271
Touchstone, 31, 41, 46, 52, 63, 65, 100, 121, 123, 126, 141, 153
Tourneur, Cyril, *The Revenger's Tragedy*, 91
Tree, Beerbohm, 72
Tree, Ellen, 76

INDEX II: SUBJECTS

Tree, Marion, 71
Trevis, Di, 68, 199, 201, 202
Tutin, Dorothy, 68, 75
Twelfth Night (act and scene)
—(1.1), 240, 256, 269
—(1.3), 222, 240
—(1.5), 238, 256, 261, 269
—(2.2), 282
—(2.3), 244, 254
—(2.4), 261
—(2.5), 220, 228, 233, 235, 237, 243, 244, 277
—(3.1), 227, 241
—(3.3), 42, 62, 264, 265, 276
—(3.4), 219, 228, 236, 246, 247, 254, 262
—(4.1), 270
—(4.2), 255, 258, 263, 286
—(5.1), 221, 229, 234, 240, 248, 249, 250, 255, 260, 276
twins, 59, 217, 221, 223, 239, 250, 251, 252, 253, 260; *see also* doubles

Universal Passion, The, 72, 156; *see also* Miller, James

Viola, 29, 36, 51, 54, 63, 64, 71, 76, 221, 226, 229, 230, 232, 233, 234, 239, 252, 258, 262, 264, 268, 273, 278, 282

Warning for Fair Women, A, 61
Washington, Denzel, 198
Waterston, Sam, 194
Webster, John, *The White Devil*, 91; *The Duchess of Malfi*, 91
Weimann, Robert, 198
Whetstone, George, *Rocke of Regard*, 157, 159
White, Richard Grant, 173
Whythorne, Thomas, 231
Widdoes, Kathleen, 194
William, 65, 100
Williams, Clifford, 134
wit, 41, 49, 169, 174, 180, 188
Woffington, Peg, 74, 156
Wynyard, Diana, 75

Zefferelli, Franco, 199

PEGASUS SHAKESPEARE BIBLIOGRAPHIES

The Pegasus Shakespeare Bibliographies — to total 12 volumes — provide handy and authoritative guides to Shakespeare scholarship and criticism. They are prepared for faculty and students in universities and colleges, as well as in high schools. Edited by leading scholar/teachers of Shakespeare, each volume is organized for ease of use. There are approximately 250 entries per volume of 160 pages; these have been selected as the best and most useful books and essays. The editors include only work of high quality or significant influence; partisanship is carefully avoided.

Most importantly, the annotations are full and helpful. The editors describe each item clearly so that a reader can quickly tell whether a particular essay or book would be useful. Cross-references and rich indexes complement the convenient organization of entries. So, with minimal effort, a reader will be able to find the right critical or scholarly resources. Additionally, the full annotations provide a good grasp of Shakespeare criticism and scholarship.

THE BOOKS ARE EMINENTLY USER-FRIENDLY, AND THE LOW PRICE ($9.95 PER VOLUME) IS FANTASTIC!

Each volume includes most or all of the following sections:
- Editions and Reference Works
- Authorship, Dating, Textual Studies
- Influences; Sources; Historical and Intellectual Backgrounds
- Language and Linguistics
- Criticism
- Stage History and Performance Criticism
- Reception History
- Adaptations
- Teaching and Collections of Essays
- Bibliographies
- Author & Subject Indexes

Send orders to our distributor—
Cornell University Press Services
750 Cascadilla Street
PO Box 6525
Ithaca, New York 14851
Email: orderbook@cupserv.org

PEGASUS SHAKESPEARE BIBLIOGRAPHIES

Volumes in Print

Love's Labor's Lost, A Midsummer Night's Dream, and The Merchant of Venice. Ed. Clifford Chalmers Huffman (1995) 0-86698-177-2

King Lear and Macbeth. Ed. Rebecca W. Bushnell (1996) 1-889818-00-3

Shakespeare and the Renaissance Stage to 1616 / Shakespearean Stage History 1616 to 1998. Ed. Hugh Macrae Richmond (1999) 1-889818-22-4

Richard II, 1 and 2 Henry IV, and Henry V. Ed. Joseph Candido (1998) 1-889818-10-0

Hamlet. Ed. Michael E. Mooney (1999) 1-889818-21-6

The Rape of Lucrece, Titus Andronicus, Julius Caesar, Antony and Cleopatra, and Coriolanus. Ed. Clifford Chalmers Huffman and John W. Velz (2002) 1-889818-30-5

Cymbeline, The Winter's Tale, and The Tempest. Ed. John S. Mebane (2002) 1-889818-31-3

Shakespeare: Life, Language & Linguistics, Textual Studies, and The Canon. Ed. Michael Warren (2002) 1-889818-34-8

As You Like It, Much Ado About Nothing, and Twelfth Night, or What You Will. Ed. Marilyn L. Williamson (2003) 1-889818-35-6

Volumes in Preparation

Jean Howard on Shakespeare criticism and literary theory

Jill Levenson on *Romeo and Juliet* and *Othello*

Barbara Traister on *Troilus and Cressida, Measure for Measure,* and *All's Well That Ends Well*

Price for each volume: $9.95.
Discounts for standing orders.

AS YOU LIKE IT, MUCH ADO ABOUT NOTHING, AND TWELFTH NIGHT, OR WHAT YOU WILL

Shakespeare's middle comedies present rich challenges to both reader and playgoer, challenges which are impressively met in this ninth volume of the Pegasus Shakespeare Bibliographies. The main challenges are posed by *Much Ado* and *Twelfth Night*—plays which, delightful as they are, sometimes arouse conflicting emotions. The volume as a whole follows the scheme of the series (described on the previous pages)—careful selection of entries, insistence on high quality or significant influence, full, clear, and useful annotations, detailed indexes, and more.

MARILYN L. WILLIAMSON, the editor of this ninth volume, is Distinguished Professor of English Emerita from Wayne State University. She has held a fellowship at the Radcliffe Institute, the AAUW Michigan Fellowship, and the J. N. Keal Chair at Wayne. Professor Williamson's publications include: *Infinite Variety: Anthony and Cleopatra in Renaissance Drama and Earlier Traditions*; *The Patriarchy of Shakespeare's Comedies*, and *Raising Their Voices: Women Writing 1640–1750*.